MADE IN SWEDEN

Elisabeth Åsbrink is a journalist and author. Her parents were Hungarian and English, and she was born and raised in, and now lives in, Sweden. Her previous books have won the August Prize, the Danish-Swedish Cultural Fund Prize, and Poland's Kapuscinski Prize. *1947* (the first of her books to be published in English, by Scribe in 2017) won the prestigious Letterstedt Prize, was translated into 19 languages, and was published in the UK, Australia, the USA, Italy, France, Germany, Spain, Brazil, South Korea, Poland, Denmark, Finland, and Norway, among others. Her latest book is *Made in Sweden*.

Scribe Publications

18–20 Edward St, Brunswick, Victoria 3056, Australia
2 John St, Clerkenwell, London, WC1N 2ES, United Kingdom
3754 Pleasant Ave, Suite 100, Minneapolis, Minnesota 55409, USA

First published in Swedish as *Orden som formade Sverige* by Natur & Kultur in 2018

This edition published by Scribe in 2019

Text and translation copyright © Elisabeth Åsbrink 2019

Excerpt from 'Prelude' by Tomas Tranströmer, translated by Rika Lesser (copyright © Rika Lesser). Reprinted by permission of Words Without Borders.

Typeset in Berling Nova Sans by the publishers
Illustrations by Allison Colpoys

Printed and bound in the UK by CPI Group (UK) Ltd, Croydon CR0 4YY

Scribe Publications is committed to the sustainable use of natural resources and the use of paper products made responsibly from those resources.

9781912854011 (UK edition)
9781925849097 (Australian edition)
9781947534841 (US edition)
9781925693706 (e-book)

Catalogue records for this book are available from the National Library of Australia and the British Library.

scribepublications.co.uk
scribepublications.com.au
scribepublications.com

ELISABETH ÅSBRINK

MADE IN SWEDEN

25 IDEAS
THAT CREATED
A COUNTRY

SCRIBE

Melbourne • London

CONTENTS

PREFACE

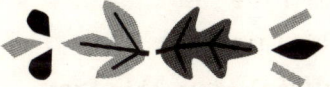

It took twenty-three years, uncountable questions during my adolescence about my origins, and one visit to Egypt for me to understand that I was, in fact, Swedish. Sort of.

Born in Sweden — even made in Sweden, according to my parents — but with a British mother and a Hungarian father, this wasn't obvious, for me or, apparently, for those around me. 'Where do you come from?' I was asked again and again, as a girl growing up in Stockholm. As I usually tell the truth, I answered, 'Gothenburg', Sweden's second biggest city. Sometimes this was considered acceptable, sometimes not. I only knew by the next line in this rather alienating conversation: 'Really?'

I never knew how they had spotted me. My name sounded Swedish enough, I didn't have an accent. Could it have been my hair? I still haven't got a clue. Something foreign transmitted from me, something atypical. It followed me wherever I went, and I cried. All I ever wanted was to look like Agnetha from ABBA.

Then a friend invited me to Sohag, in Egypt. She asked me to visit her class of English students — they rarely come across westerners, she said, and it would be good for them to practise their English on me. Fine. I was twenty-three at the time and the students were maybe eighteen or nineteen, a group of men and women with bright eyes. One of them, a girl, started the session by asking, 'When you marry, is it because of love or because of money?'

And there I was, hearing myself explaining the basics of my existence, all the structural, legal, and cultural ground I had beneath my feet — women in my country's rights to work, inherit, use childcare, be independent — everything that made me able to marry for love. The students listened carefully and nodded with great interest. All of a sudden, I became aware of my Swedishness. Up until then, I had only known my strangeness.

Today, Scandinavia is trendy. The word 'hygge' has escaped from Denmark and travelled the world, promoting the Danish idea of happiness and ignoring the high usage of anti-depressants there. Something similar is going on with the Swedish word 'lagom'. In a race with other Swedish identity concepts of an older sort, like IKEA, meatballs, Roxette, and Zlatan Ibrahimović, the concept of 'lagom' has completely taken over. I even heard it mentioned on the BBC television series *Shetland* the other day. It can't get more mainstream than that.

The word 'lagom' means 'enough' or 'good enough', and is used to promote Sweden as a modern, pleasant country, with good taste in design, music, and crime fiction. But actually, Sweden isn't 'lagom' at all. On the contrary, the Swedish way of living and its basic values are extreme compared to rest of the world. Ingmar Bergman being Swedish is no coincidence. Sweden is also the country which had 63,888 of its citizens forcibly sterilised — a Swedish record not many have heard about. Nothing 'lagom' about that.

By the way, I love this strange country in which I happen to have been born. But my love isn't blind. Here are 25 reasons why.

—Elisabeth Åsbrink, writer
Stockholm/Copenhagen, December 2018

SUINOM HINC CIVITAS

Suionum hinc civitates ipso in oceano praeter viros armaque classibus valent.

And now begin the states of the Suiones, situated on the Ocean itself, and these, besides men and arms, are powerful in ships.[1]

'Suionum', he wrote, the Roman historian Tacitus, in 98 AD, and by doing so, he became the first to mention the people who would become known as 'the Swedes'. Later, in ancient Anglo-Saxon literature, the word 'sweonas' appears. In the sixth century, the historian Jordanes wrote about 'suehans' as

---

1 Tacitus, Cornelius, 'Germany and its tribes', *The Complete Works of Tacitus*. Translated by Church, Alfred John and Brodribb, William Jackson, with an introduction by Hadas, Moses. New York: The Modern Library (1942). http://www.perseus.tufts.edu/hopper/text?doc=Perseus%3Atext%3A1999.02.0083%3Achapter%3D44

well as 'suetidi', and in his chronicle from the eleventh century, Adam of Bremen, a German historian, told the story about 'sueones'. At the same time, the Icelandic sagas speak of 'sviar'.

Are they all describing the same people? We have no idea. Are they Swedish? Who knows? Spurred by a general longing for logic in the random events we call history-leading-up-to-the-present, historians and nationalists use Tacitus and the others as if they were suppliers of indubitable facts, when it would be more accurate to describe them as isolated sources of light in a compact historical darkness. Or, to quote the anonymous, probably many-headed creator of the Swedish Wikipedia page about the Swedes: 'the lack of sources is massive'.

Apart from in Germanic legends and Nordic mythology — neither accepted as irrefutable grounds for accurate history writing — there is hardly any information describing the ancient Swedes. The one thing that can be said for sure is that they were a Germanic population living in the present Sweden. That's all. Nothing about where this population had their home, how widespread it was, or its development is known for sure. According to an early historical theory, the Swedes' core area was situated just north of Stockholm, from where the population expanded. However, the denominator 'Swedes' ('svear') may also have been used for a specific, demarcated layer of the population.

The ancient Swedes are often said to have been seafaring and warlike, and are sometimes posed as opposite to the

'Goths' ('goter'), another supposedly ancient group of people that may have formed the base of the present Swedish population — hence, for instance, the name of the city of Gothenburg in the west of Sweden. But, again, neither Goths nor Swedes are easily defined.

The Eastern Roman historian Jordanes wrote a chronicle of the history of the Gothic people: *De origine actibusque Getarum* (*The Origin and Deeds of the Getae/Goths*). In this, he claims that the Goths are connected to the ancient Getae people, thus bestowing on them a long and glorious history. In his work, Jordanes describes Scandinavia as the 'womb of all nations', from where the Goths emigrated and conquered most parts of the world.

This interpretation of history continued for centuries. Lines of connection were drawn between Getae — Goths — Götar (the Swedish form of 'Goths'), transforming a cold, peripheric part of the world into its cultural birthplace. A good story, but fake facts. Nevertheless, in time Jordanes' chronicle became the main source for a strong cult of Swedish self-awareness and pride.

Another historian to acknowledge the Swedes early on, as previously mentioned, was Adam of Bremen, in the eleventh century. He got most of his information from the Danish king at the time, Sven Estridsson, who used the term 'Swedes' in two different, contradictory ways: on one hand, as the name of a certain group of people, excluding the Goths; on the other, in a way that included the Goths. Some of Adam of Bremen's depictions of the old settlements in Uppsala, Birka, and Sigtuna contain details that may very well be historically correct. Others do not:

> There lies the great community of Sigtuna. In the east, it borders the Ripheic mountains, where there are vast deserts and high snowmasses, and where flocks of monstrous people hinder further intrusion. There are Amazons, people with dogs' heads, cyclopes, who have a single eye in the forehead. Furthermore, there are the creatures that Solinus calls 'himantopodes', who run on one leg, and also those who enjoy human flesh as food. That's why one should evade them and also rightly choose not to mention them.

However, at the same time as Adam of Bremen describes the Swedish cannibals, the first proof of an actual people who actually call themselves Swedes emerges — of all places in the port of Piraeus, just outside Athens, three thousand kilometres due south.

Once, there was a stone lion, sculpted in white-shimmering Pentelic marble quarried in Attica. At three metres high, the lion had been guarding the Piraeus harbour since the first century AD. Around the year 1050, a group of Scandinavian mercenaries in the service of the Byzantine Empire must have come by, laid eyes on the sculpture, and liked what they saw.

Several historical documents testify that so-called Varangians, warriors from the north, were used in the Byzantine Emperor's navy or army. Many of them had been drafted in the 1000s to crush a Bulgarian rebellion and then travelled to Piraeus to celebrate the victory. This particular group of Varangians had lost one of its men, a farmer named Horse. He had unfortunately fallen before being paid for his soldier's struggle. Many rune stones in Scandinavia had been erected to honour men with a similar fate, who had died in Greece before acquiring wealth for their heirs. To commemorate Horse, his fellow warriors decided to make their grief plain on the lion's left leg:

> they carved, the troopers ... and in this harbour, these men
> carved runes after Horse the farm-owner ... Swedes had
> this done on the lion. Fell before he could take a ransom.[2]

This translation was made a few years back by rune expert Thorgunn Snædal. She bases her interpretation on the fact that, by the ninth century, most people residing in the north had ceased to erect memorial stones, while the custom

---

2 Snædal, Thorgunn, 'Runes from Byzantium: reconsidering the Piraeus lion'. *Byzantium and the Viking world*. Edited by Androshchuk, Fedir, Shepard, Jonathan, and White, Monica. Uppsala: Uppsala Universiteit (2016).

continued to flourish in large parts of what is now Sweden. Snædal concludes that the ornamental message on the Piraeus Lion actually is the very first evidence of people who consider themselves Swedes.

Svions, sweonas, suehans, suetidi, sueones, sviar ... The words lie shimmering like silver coins in the bottom of a well and reflect light to anyone in need of a story with a beginning, a middle, and an ending. It may be the story of a people, of a language, of a country; the story of a story — then the fragments, the silver below the surface, will be of use.

Perhaps the greeting on the white marble lion in Piraeus can be read in another way? That you are what you call yourself?

2

BEOWULF

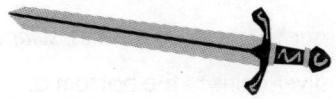

The idea of a national epic — a mythologised legendary poetical work that defines the very soul of a nation — arose in the beginning of the nineteenth century. Up until then, the long poem about the fighter Beowulf had just been another dusty manuscript lying around, not considered more valuable than any other old poem, equally dusty. But then it was 'discovered' and dubbed a national epic in England. As it takes place in Scandinavia, with a hero from what might be present-day Sweden, the poem is seen as a national epic there as well.

The fact that *Beowulf* is regarded as the oldest surviving poem in England is due to two lines of events. First, King Henry VIII destroyed the English monasteries when he broke with Catholicism and introduced the English version of the Protestant faith. As a consequence, hundreds, maybe thousands, of old manuscripts were destroyed or disappeared. But as it happened, the *Beowulf* manuscript survived. Secondly, there was a fire at Ashburnham House in Westminster in 1731, where *Beowulf* and other old manuscripts had been brought for safe-keeping. The epic poem was severely damaged, but survived, once again. We live in a cathedral of coincidences.

The poem that happened to endure when so many others did not was transcribed into modern English in 1805 and has since been ceaselessly subjected to interpretations, research, and grand conclusions. Ten years later, it was translated into Latin and Danish by the writer N.S.F. Grundtvig, amongst others, and thus became central in both the Danish and Swedish search for an original self.

Its 3,182 lines depict how the monster Grendel is disturbed at night by the partying going on in the royal hall of Danish King Hrothgar. Joyful singing is especially painful for Grendel, and one night he attacks the party and kills thirty of the king's men. He then returns each night for the following twelve years, keeping the situation under his monster thumb. In the south of Sweden, a great Geatish man called Beowulf hears of the sorry state of affairs in Denmark, and sails off to help. Beowulf wrestles with Grendel in the banqueting hall and drives the monster away. But then Grendel's mother comes to seek vengeance. She kills Beowulf's closest comrades, but he tracks her back to her home swamp and kills her there. Beowulf is rewarded for his help by the Danish court, sails home, and becomes king of the Geats until he fights a dragon and is slain.

While the Danish state tourism websites use the *Beowulf* saga to get people to visit Viking museums, the Swedes claim that the poem contains the first mention of an actual Swedish country, 'Swīorīce'.

But the mystery of location lingers; where does the whole Beowulf story take place? According to the Icelandic sagas, the Danish royal family — to which King Hrothgar belonged — resided in the small village of Lejre, less than a mile from the city of Roskilde. This was long before Denmark was christened and became a medieval kingdom. When archaeologists have done excavations in Lejre, they've actually revealed impressive remains of what could be the great royal feasting hall at the epicentre of the *Beowulf* story.

In Sweden, the dispute has focused on Beowulf and his people, the Geats. Who were they? Should they be considered Swedish? Three peoples are mentioned in the poem: Danes, Jutes, and Geats. Researchers have identified the Danes as, hmm, the Danes, and the Jutes as people from Jutland (nowadays a part of Denmark), but the Geats remain a mystery. In a purely etymological sense there is a line between the Anglo-Saxon word 'geatas' and the Swedish folk name 'götar', and according to that linguistic logic Beowulf and his people would have come from the area called Götaland in Sweden. Or not.

On the Municipality of Gotland's website it is stated that Beowulf was a 'gute' — that is, originating from the island Gotland. The statement is reinforced by an archaeologist who sailed from Gotland to Denmark and hereby believes he has proven the two-day route Beowulf took. Everyone wants a piece of the *Beowulf* cake.

The *Iliad* and *Odyssey* became in-demand in connection with the Greek independence war in the 1820s and have been ever since, just as *The Tale of Igor's Campaign* came to play a major role when Russian nationalism was puffed up in connection with the Napoleonic Wars. In France, *The Song of Roland* is considered a national epic; the Germans have their *Nibelungenlied*, the Finns have *Kalevala*, the Poles have *Pan Tadeusz*, and so on. In a national epic, the spirit of the nation is expressed, it is said. But often enough there is also a sense of superiority and an awakening of some kind of legendary birthright. And now, what do we have? A hundred-year-old discussion about *Beowulf* comprising part of the Swedish national origin story. Why?

Could it have to do with a need for solid anchoring in a time when so much seems floating and approximate? Or is it about the power of literature, of images of courage and brutal violence? Or might the sustained fascination for *Beowulf* depend on the world's disorder, and the relief when a powerful figure arises to set everything right — a saviour who stops the world's relentless ongoing self-destruction? Whatever the answer, *Beowulf* is still going strong.

3

DANISH BASTARDS

In the autumn of 1449, the Franciscan friars in the monastery on the small island now called Riddarholmen in Stockholm wrote a song on behalf of King Karl Knutsson. It was not that the king didn't like the Danes — he had several Danish family members and could certainly see himself as King of Denmark if he ever got the opportunity — but there's a difference between one's private life and the quest for power.

The monks served as a propaganda centre. They had already contributed to the king's self-reverence in several rhymed chronicles, and now they wrote Gotlandsvisan (the Gotland song) at his demand, 28 verses of hatred directed at the Danes. Many Swedes can still quote the lines:

Danish men's words
Are worse than murder

Karl Knutsson was a power-hungry man. During his lifetime, he managed to be crowned Swedish king three times and Norwegian king once. Of course, his hateful propaganda against the Danes was based on the desire to conquer land and kingdom, but not for the sake of a nation, just for himself.

The borders between Sweden and Denmark were still undrawn, the nation state an idea no one had yet thought of. During the Middle Ages, war was conducted out of royal desire for greater power and territories; it was not a question of one country taking on another. Danish kings raided southern Sweden and vice versa; Swedish regents plundered the (then) Danish areas of Skåne and Blekinge. At this particular moment in time, the most desirable piece of land of them all was the island of Gotland. There, in the medieval city of Visby, a Nordic ex-king had settled in the castle.

Erik of Pomerania had once ruled over Norway, Sweden, and Denmark, but now he was king only of the pirates robbing the ships that passed by. The situation in *annus* 1448 can thus be summarised in three sentences: The Danish regent wanted Gotland. The Swedish regent wanted Gotland. The ex-regent Erik had it.

Karl Knutsson made an attempt to invade the island as soon as he became the king of Sweden. The rural areas were taken without difficulty, and soon Swedish troops also gained control over the island's main city, Visby. But the castle, where

Erik of Pomerania had holed up, wouldn't give way. Erik was out of reach, but he was also trapped. He sent a message to the Danish king requesting help, and just a few days later the Danish navy arrived to drive every single Swede from the island. That's when King Karl Knutsson ordered the monks in Stockholm to write *Gotlandsvisan*, in which the Danes are described as deceitful and lying scorpions.

Us and them. Them and us. There is no doubt that the Swedish hatred of the Danes was a result of a small number of Swedish families' attempts to extend influence for themselves. Through vilifying thy neighbour, land can be claimed.

A hundred years later, in the middle of the sixteenth century, the historian Johannes Magnus published the great chronicle of Swedish kings *Historia de omnibus gothorum sveonumque regibus*, in which he claims that the ruling Vasa family were derived from the biblical Noah's grandson Magog. According to Magnus' chronicle, Magog travelled to Sweden eighty-eight years after the flood, settled there because of the good availability of fish and game, and began breeding Swedish royalty. The scripture goes on to prove that Sweden is the oldest and most prominent country of all the countries in the world.

Needless to say, this chronicle became extremely popular. The Vasa family now had its right to the crown, power, and supremacy firmly established in the archaic stories of the Holy Bible. This way of counting kings all the way back to Noah's son Magog still affects what numbers Swedish regents are given today. The present king is called Karl the sixteenth, even though there haven't been fifteen Karls before him — unless, of course, you see the world through *Historia de omnibus gothorum sveonumque regibus*.

In this immensely influential text, there is also a crucial part concerning the Danes. The way the Danish talk, look, and sound is meticulously described, as well as deeply despised. They lie, swear, eat mouldy bread, drink bad beer, and are compared to angry trolls.

Over the centuries, the antipathy between the two kingdoms became ominous. In connection with the Northern Seven Years' War — with Sweden on one side and Denmark, Lübeck, and Poland on the other — numerous propaganda pamphlets were distributed by both sides. When the time came for a peace treaty in 1570, the hate speech was considered so damning and dangerous that it was separately proscribed. In the documents regulating the peace it stated that those many nefarious scriptures had underpinned the enmity between Sweden and Denmark and contributed to prolonging the war. As such pamphlets could easily spark further disagreement and acts of war, the two kings guaranteed neither to print nor distribute them, and any of their subjects defying the rule were to be punished by death. All existing pamphlets were confiscated and destroyed.

Peace prevailed, but so did contempt. In Denmark, for instance, the verb 'Swedish' was, as late as the 1830s, synonymous with being deceitful or a thief.

At the turn of the twentieth century, the Swedish scientist Gustav Sundbärg wrote a book to establish a Swedish 'national character'. In order to demonstrate Swedish features, he described the Danish as the opposite. Self-image, counter-image — the one inevitably reflected the other. In his book, the Danes are compared with Swedes in all possible aspects of life. Strangely enough, almost all comparisons turn out in favour of the Swedish national character.

> ... when the Swede really has to think something through, the result usually is more profound and more distinctive than when a Dane thinks. Indeed, the Swede is very often a very talented thinker, and almost always his views are broader than those of the Dane. Just take a look at the large and high foreheads that are so common among the Swedes, really made for thinking. They represent large and clean lines of thought, as opposed to the Danes' clever, curly spirals. How frequently this shows in the face of a Dane, which is often almost painfully twisted and distorted. Despite being very clever, the Danish rarely come up with anything dramatically innovative.

Gustav Sundbärg's book became a bestseller, was published in several editions, and was received with great appreciation at home. In Denmark, the literature critic Harald Nielsen wrote an answer, the book 'Dansk og Svensk' (Danish and Swedish), where he pretty much did the same thing but from a Danish point of view:

> From my childhood, I remember that most people perceived Swedes as insidious. This was not, however, based on any historical memory, but on the impressions made by Swedish workers, and the contradiction between the silent, the reserved, and the brooding aspects of their character in comparison with the easy-going and talkative Danes. When you least of all expected it — and the Danes had already forgotten all about it — this Swedish silence could turn into a violent outbreak.

And so it goes on, a continuing mirroring across the cold blue of Öresund, the marine strait which forms the Swedish-Danish border; one country sees its advantages by formulating the flaws of the other. It affects how the public conversation is conducted in each country: the views on women and sexuality, the location of nuclear power plants, or the degrees of xenophobia. Whatever the subject, we are always better than them. No wonder the mutual state of antipathy lingers on, trickling into politics, art, and everyday life. Lars von Trier's television series *The Kingdom* would be nothing without it. Who can ever forget the Swedish main character standing on a rooftop in Copenhagen in the night, looking over to the Swedish side, lights glittering across the dark waters of Öresund, declaring:

> Here Denmark: shat out of chalk and water. And there,
> Sweden: hewn from granite. Danish bastards! Danish
> bastards!

4

THE SACRED NATURE

Now comes the time of blooming
With beauty and great joy
You now draw near, sweet summer
Soon crops and grass will grow
With warmth of gentle glowing
To all that's been withdrawn
The sun's rays are oncoming
And the world will be re-born

Hymn number 199 in the Swedish Hymnal is the soundtrack to a kaleidoscopic collective memory where lilacs are in bloom, children are dressed in white, and headmasters tediously render up praise and thanks for the blessings of the year gone by. The hymn is sung in classrooms, school halls, and churches around the country at the beginning of every June, when the spring term comes to an end and two months of summer leave begins. Something is concluded: a term, a work effort, days of safe monotony or of insecure misery, and the shift can neither be hurried nor halted. The hymn marks departure as well as continuity, and as such it becomes a portal to the summer.

Nobody knows for sure where the melody originally came from. Is it German or Norwegian? Maybe, maybe not. The hymnologists' debate about the hymn's origins isn't that interesting. The question is rather why the song awakens such great feelings of love in Swedes. What makes 'Now comes the time of blooming' Sweden's most beloved hymn, when the rest of the Nordic countries (except Iceland) unreservedly vote for 'Härlig är Jorden' ('Fair is creation')? Is the deeply felt relief of leaving school for the summer reason enough? Or is it because the religious message is of a lighter, joyful kind? Or is the reason simply nature? Because a lot of things in Sweden can be explained with nature. The simple fact of giving the kids two months of summer leave is explained with nature.

In the agricultural society of the old days, children couldn't be occupied with school in times of sowing, taking care of the crops, and harvesting. They were needed in the fields, taking care of the farm animals and of whatever the earth gave. In the nineteenth century, when a majority of the Swedish hymns were composed, this was simply common sense and the natural cycle of life. Uncountable Swedish hymns depict God as nature: flowers, trees, meadows, green fields, the sun's warmth, and, not to forget, animals, are recurring themes. In the Swedish Hymnal from 1937 you find pigeons, swallows, butterflies, and fish. The birds are mentioned twenty-three times. In the 1986 edition, these creatures have been joined by 'the ant with the straw, striving / the eagle in space, hovering'. Even if nature also featured in the first Christian hymns, the sun, the stars and the birds there were metaphoric, representing the passing of time. They were never God in disguise. It's worth noting that up until about 400 AD, Christianity had been a purely urban phenomenon. The Latin word for pagan, for instance — *paganus* — actually means villager.

But something happened to the Christian God when he or she arrived in the Nordic part of the world. The Catholic missionaries understood that, if the new faith was to be meaningful to people who lived at the mercy of the weather, depended on the harvest, and whatever else the earth, the woods, and the waters might give, the Christian message must be adapted — to nature.

Maybe it all comes down to such basics as infrastructure, geography, and a comparatively small population. These parameters simply had to be taken into consideration in a region where there were more forests than churches, more undeveloped land than settlements, more hills than cities. People simply had to carry their faith with them wherever they were. And then, with the advent of the Reformation and the new idea of a direct relationship with God — with no priest or congregation as intermediary — the individual worshippers became even more free to seek spirituality in their own way and in places of their own choosing. Hence the forest paths became holy, the shores of lakes turned into prayer rooms, and the crops in the fields became greetings and gifts from a higher power.

I'll be fine. I am sitting on a rock by a lake in a forest.
I need some time for myself.

In the song 'A stone by a lake in the woods', Per Gessle from the pop duo Roxette defines what can be considered a very Swedish value, at least if one is to believe a sociological study from 2015[3]. When over 2,000 people diagnosed with cancer were asked how they coped with their situation, 68 per cent of the Swedish respondents replied that they turned to nature to seek comfort. Only 14 per cent chose the church. Listening to hymns or religious music appealed to 14 per cent, while 66 per cent preferred birdsong and the sound of the wind in the trees. The conclusion by the researcher behind the study is that Sweden is unique in this aspect: nothing is holier to Swedes than nature itself.

---

3   Ahmadi, Fereshteh, and Ahmadi, Nader, 'Meaning-making Methods for Coping with Serious Illness', *Studies in Secular and Religious Societies*, London: Routledge (2018).

As for 'Now comes the time of blooming', it was first published in 1694 but received such criticism from the bishops of Sweden that it was supposed to be withdrawn from publication. The clergy didn't feel it conveyed the message of God clearly enough and — far worse — the hymn confused worldly joy with spiritual joy. With lyrics like 'Make love burn in heart, renew soul and mind' or 'Impregnate earth with dew so she'll have the delightful scent of a Lebanese rose' their point is easily understood.

Even so, the hymn remained in the official Swedish Hymnal, re-written but still quite focused on the sensual world. Thus 'Now comes the time of blooming' was saved for the euphoria or despair of leaving school for the summer, and deeply entangled with the delicate scent of lilacs in bloom, the gathering outside schools of children dressed in white, the underlined emptiness of school buildings during leave (no other buildings are ever that empty), and the almost petrifying hope and unspoken expectations that the summer ahead of you might hold something in store you never even knew you desired, something of beauty and great joy.

5

HOMO SAPIENS

As early as March 1753, Carl Nilsson Linnæus complained about his workload. Later on, when he had been knighted and changed his name to Carl von Linnaeus, he again brought up this grievance. In 1761, he wrote to a friend:

> I lecture every day for an hour in public and afterwards
> give private instruction to a number of pupils ... Having
> thus talked for five hours before lunch, in the afternoon
> I correct work, prepare my manuscripts for the printers
> and write letters to my botanical friends, visit the garden
> and deal with people who want to consult me ... with the
> result that often I hardly have a moment to eat ... While
> my colleagues daily enjoy the pleasures of this existence,
> I spend days and nights in the exploration of a field of
> learning that thousands of them will not suffice to bring

to completion, not to mention that every day I have to
squander time on correspondence with various scholars
— all of which will age me prematurely.[4]

There was so much knowledge he had already acquired
and yet still so much more that remained to be discovered
— and all of it needed to be organised, noted, sorted, and
then entered in tables, charts, publications, footnotes, and
lectures. Risk of burnout, one might say. But work itself wasn't
the only thing stressing him out — he was also under pressure
for the same reasons people get burned out nowadays: information overload.

In the Linnean Society offices in London, one can find
his collection of biological samples of 14,300 plants, 168 fish,
3,000 shellfish, and 3,198 insects, as well as a library of 1,600
books and over 4,000 letters and manuscripts. At the pinna-
cle of his career, Linnaeus was the centre of a tight network
of correspondence covering Europe and beyond. Friends
and researchers sent him new discoveries at the same time
as they discussed, criticised, and supplemented the old. He
had a number of adepts, so-called apostles, whom he sent on
assignments around the world, to Russia, the Middle East, West

4   Müller-Wille, Staffan and Charmantier, Isabelle, 'Natural history and information overload:
The case of Linnaeus', 'Studies in History and Philosophy of Science Part C: Studies in History
and Philosophy of Biological and Biomedical Sciences', Volume 43, Issue 1, March 2012, pages
4–15 https://www.sciencedirect.com/science/article/pii/S1369848611001130

Africa, and China, and who reported home in letters, and sent books and biological samples. And all of it had to be sorted into the correct botanical genera, checked against previously received information, named, updated, and classified. Carl von Linnaeus worked day and night.

His motto was *Omnia mirari etiam tritissima* — Marvel at everything, even the commonplace. But there is nothing commonplace about his achievement within natural science. Over a hundred years ahead of Charles Darwin presenting his theory of evolution, Linnaeus made it possible by thinking the unthinkable when he classified the human being as a primate and sorted her into the same family as the monkey. In order to distinguish humans from other mammals, he invented a special description: *Homo sapiens*, the knowledgeable man. In spite of this distinction, academics and theologians were outraged by the shocking act of equating the image of God with a monkey's.

Linnaeus certainly believed in God. But his starting point was that, although God had created all living things, there existed a hierarchical structure in the world and it was Linnaeus' mission to uncover it. By doing so, he opened a line of thought for Charles Darwin to develop a scientific truth in which both nature itself and human evolution could be explained without God. (By the way, Darwin considered Carl von Linnaeus as one of his three gods, side by side with the French fossilist Georges Cuvier, and, of course, Aristotle.)

Linnaeus had been on the verge of burnout for years. Visitors to his hometown of Uppsala described him as unshaven, with dusty shoes and socks, wearing an old green smock. But there were things to be solved. He who organised God's Nature lacked a good method of organising. Already in the 1750s, when he had sorted the Swedish queen's collection of butterflies, he had experimented with paper cards. One of his colleagues then travelled to London and organised Sloane's Collection at the British Museum according to Linnaeus' principle. However, the system that had worked for a collection of butterflies did not suffice for all the various pieces of knowledge and facts that continually swept towards him from the world. God created, Linnaeus sorted. For this purpose he needed an adjustable structure, where he could easily add new knowledge and just as easily erase inaccuracies; it ought to be possible to arrange it linearly, chronologically, alphabetically, or whichever way he wanted. Around 1767, he began using a system of thick paper cards; thousands of cards of the same size. They could be stored in boxes, sorted, provide information that led to other cards and thereby could tie his body of research together. In short, he created a searchable system of information he could easily supervise.

He might have been inspired by playing cards. In his time, the back of the card was left blank for notes to be made, and many researchers and academics used them much in the same way we now use post-its. (Playing cards have been found beneath the floorboards of the Linnaeus home.) Whatever the case, he invented the index card, according to research by Isabelle Charmantier of the Linnean Society and Professor Staffan Müller-Wille from the Centre for Medical History at the University of Exeter.[5] Not until 1780, two years after Linnaeus' death, did Vienna's Court Library introduce a card catalogue, the first of its kind.[6]

Homo sapiens is the knowledgeable human being; the fact-gathering, perceptive creature who seeks to broaden the world by naming, arranging, and understanding it. Thus it was himself Carl von Linnaeus named, sorted, and catalogued. Just as he observed the world, he observed himself, and no one personified *Homo sapiens* like him. As a result, Sweden (and the rest of the world) was left with a legacy of structuring reality through records, accounts, and lists. Criminal records, telephone databases, death records, birth records, property records, drug records, Windrush landing-cards records, tax records, just to mention a few.

5   Müller-Wille, Staffan and Charmantier, Isabelle, 'Carl Linnaeus's botanical paper slips (1767–1773)', 'Intellectual History Review', Volume 24, Issue 2, 2014, pages 215–238 https://www.tandfonline.com/doi/pdf/10.1080/17496977.2014.914643

6   Blei, Daniela, 'How the Index Card Cataloged the World', *The Atlantic*, 1 December 2017 https://www.theatlantic.com/technology/archive/2017/12/how-the-index-card-catalogued-the-world/547271/

6

SWEDISH VALUES
IN THE MAKING

A vast amount of information about human beliefs and values in almost a hundred countries, collected by an international group of social scientists, is presented in the World Values Survey 2015[7]. Based on interviews with almost 400,000 respondents, the study suggests that Swedish values differ significantly from those of the rest of the world.

In the Nordic countries in general — and in Sweden specifically — individual autonomy is emphasised very strongly, while residents show a great degree of confidence in both their fellow human beings and the authorities in a way that distinctively differs from the rest of the world. It's actually possible to blame one single man for the extreme Swedish stand in the world of

---

7   http://www.worldvaluessurvey.org/wvs.jsp

human values — that is the writer Carl Jonas Love Almqvist. It's in his troubled soul some crucial Swedish values first appear.

Carl Jonas Love Almqvist was an imaginative writer and a sharp-pencilled journalist at work in the early years of the nineteenth century. He was unhappily married and longed for love and for sex. In addition, Almqvist longed for a life in the midst of nature, for God, and he yearned for worldly success. He also dreamed of a society governed by a different set of rules and of a love that was free to follow its own laws of desire, friendship, and loneliness, and of all his dreams and yearnings, maybe this dream went deeper and became the strong undercurrent influencing the rest.

In 1839, at the age of 46, he published a short novel, *Det går an* (translated into English as *Sara Videbeck and the Chapel*). It's a story about Sara, the daughter of a glazier, and the non-commissioned officer Albert, both in their early twenties. They meet by chance on a steamboat trip and a relationship takes form. Reading it today, the novel seems almost without incident, but for the Swedish society at the time it was more than enough. The plot was considered outrageous. It is indicated that the couple have sex. Every step taken to deepen the relationship is taken by the woman. There are even signs of her experiencing an orgasm. The good Swedes were deeply shocked, and Almqvist was accused of spreading immoral ideas.

But putting the sexual aspects of the novel aside, an even more revolutionary narrative appears, one of greater future significance: Sara wants to be free. She wants a professional life, economic independence, and self-sufficiency. She has witnessed her mother helplessly go down, beaten by her husband and made penniless by his alcoholism. Sara has decided never to surrender to a similar fate and has decided to never ever marry. Almqvist lets his female protagonist plan her life with Albert without them becoming husband and wife. Instead, the couple should keep separate households and have separate finances. He can move in with her, but on condition that he rents a room. Then they'll help each other, spend time together, and love each other out of free will, not because the marital institution so demands.

In the fierce public debate that followed, critics accused the novel's female character of being everything short of a prostitute. As a result of the scandal, Almqvist eventually lost his job as headmaster of a reputable school in Stockholm.

But there are several layers to his short, seemingly simple book. It also deals with society's general lack of love. Almqvist was not amoral. On the contrary, he was deeply convinced that intercourse without love was more immoral than intercourse without marriage. He took the same stance concerning matrimony. If it wasn't based on love, it was just as immoral

— or actually worse — than love without marriage. The church demanding chastity up until the wedding night prevented people from getting to know each other in all senses — leading to mismatches and unhappy marriages.

Even if his readers recognised the problems he described, the general morale did not allow such an opinion to be expressed in public debate. Almqvist was heavily criticised and ridiculed, and not only by the 'public' and the church. He also made women who aspired to gender equality furious. They considered Sara to be a male fantasy: an independent woman who did not make a claim of duty of any man but still was willing to share her bed with a man, who provided free access to love and sex but let him off the hook when it came to economic, legal, or moral obligations. An unmarried woman in the Sweden of 1839 who behaved like this would be completely unprotected, without support for herself or her children. Besides, she would be exposed to society's contempt and alienation. What Almqvist dreamed about was not possible. At least, not yet.

What did Carl Jonas Love Almqvist actually wish to achieve with his challenging novel? An answer can be found in another book, *Det Europeiska missnöjets grunder* (*Grounds for European Discontent*), which he wrote a decade later. There he develops the idea of a new social order. Visions of love and happiness still constitute his driving forces, but are now placed in a political context where major entities in society must be transformed;

the family, parish life, and, above all, marriage itself must be changed. The freedom of the individual was to be safeguarded. The woman must be economically independent, and the status of children must be secured through inheritance tax and a 'child insurance authority'.

A strong ideal of individualism was his starting point, paired with a democratic stance, ensuring each and every person the same right to search for freedom and happiness, regardless of gender and social class — because true love can only happen between two individuals who are completely independent. In other words, Swedish values today.

Almqvist was no solitary thinker in a desolate Europe. He was influenced by writers like Jean-Jacques Rousseau, Wolfgang von Goethe, and Friedrich Schiller, who all raised questions concerning the idea of love and love's practice in the 1800s. Although Almqvist's books did not lead to any immediate political changes, he made the first crack in the tight patriarchal structure that would eventually crumble and be replaced by parliamentarism and liberal reforms.

His ideas concerning the protection of children were later developed by the Swedish author and women's ideologist Ellen Key, and then further developed and put into political practice by the influential social democrat Alva Myrdal in the 1930s. In order to make it possible for women to work and become inde-pendent of their husbands, Myrdal suggested state day-care centres where children between the ages of two and seven could stay while their mothers worked. There they could play and be fostered and thus receive opportunities not all families would be able to give them.

Almqvist's vision was a state that ensured individual citizens security and happiness on a liberal basis. A hundred years later, the Social Democratic party made it happen. Children and women would be entitled to separate state support, thereby guaranteeing that the children were given as decent an upbringing as possible, regardless of whether their father was out of work or an alcoholic.

And this is Sweden today. When an individual becomes ill, old, or weak, he or she doesn't have to depend on the family for help, but instead turns to the state directly. If a child is maltreated or abused, authorities take responsibility. If you are broke, authorities support you. If you are unemployed or disabled, society takes responsibility. The state controls children's education and hands out cheap loans so no one should be forced to refrain from university studies because of their parents' financial situation.

Similar welfare structures are found in the other Nordic countries, but nowhere else has the direct link between individual and state evolved as far as in Sweden. When the movement for gender equality was first sparked in the 1960s, it was as if Almqvist's words echoed in the public debate: 'A prerequisite for gender equality is that women become fully economical and socially independent of men.'

In the 1970s, the vision became Swedish reality. The individual was ultimately freed from family dependence when the Swedish government introduced separate taxation for husband and wife. (In France, Greece, Ireland, Luxembourg, Malta, the Netherlands, Poland, Portugal, Switzerland, Spain, the Baltic countries, and Germany for instance, married couples are jointly taxed.) As of 1977, parents were not obliged to support their children after their eighteenth birthday and children were no longer obliged to support their elderly parents if they lacked income in old age; the state would take responsibility.

But there is a dark side to Utopia. Freedom from family ties and obligations also creates alienation. Independence creates solitude. The result is a state-regulated system that lays the foundation for the famous Swedish melancholy.

7

HERE'S THE FIRST

Here's the first

Sing hup fol-de-rol la la la la

Here's the first

Sing hup fol-de-rol la la

He who doesn't drink the first

Shall never, ever quench his thirst

Here's the first!

[drink]

Sing hup fol-de-rol la la!

When Scandinavians want to party like the Swedes, they raise their glasses and sing the first line of 'Helan går' ('Here's the first'). That does the trick. They then go back to getting drunk in the normal way.

The first three notes of the drinking song — e, g, and c

— sound bright and challenging, a signal to interrupt-whatever-you're-doing-and-listen-up! It's easy to imagine a trumpeter in an army band playing them as a fanfare. Some time around the turn of the century, someone put words to the melody and 'Here's the first' became as popular as drinking itself. (Even though the Swedish capital at the time only had a population of 70,000 people, there were around 700 pubs.)

The first time the drinking song is noted in a historical context was on stage in an opera by Frans Berwald in 1845. It turned out the drinking song wasn't considered classy enough for the jewel-rattling audience. The orchestra obstructed it by drumming their bows on the music stands and that was the end of that. No one ever heard anything of that opera again. Not that 'Here's the first' lost its power — far from it. Forty years later, the writer August Strindberg rhetorically asked if it was not in fact Sweden's true national anthem. In an essay called 'I Bernadottes land' ('Bernadotte's country') he described how respectable men stood up at dinner parties and with serious dedication sang their hearts out: 'It is a strange sight to see the director-general of the national heritage board, the university professor, the theatre manager and the member of the Royal Swedish Academy turn into young boys.'

Another fifty years later, the Hungarian-Austrian composer Franz Lehár made a similar observation. When his operetta *The Merry Widow* was to be performed in Stockholm in 1936, he visited the city and was wined and dined by the cultural stars of the time as well as business executives. After a dinner at Operakällaren — the 'in' place at the time — when all the men in evening dress present stood up with grave faces and burst into 'Here's the first', Lehár was convinced he had heard the Swedish national anthem. And he liked it. Back in Vienna he composed five variations on the theme, so the drinking song now exists in a minor key as a Viennese waltz.

Ironically, the idea of the drinking song as national anthem actually came true. At the Ice Hockey World Cup final in 1957, the Swedish team played against the Soviet Union and defeated them. But the organisers hadn't taken a Swedish victory into account and subsequently hadn't brought a gramophone record with the Swedish anthem to play during the prize ceremony. There they were, the winners of the World Cup, represented by the Swedish player Lasse Björn, standing at the top of the prize pool with Czechs and Russians on each side below and no national anthem to be found — what was he supposed to do? He chose the one song he was sure the whole team could sing by heart. And while they sang, the legendary Soviet Marshal Zhukov, who had won the battle of Stalingrad and taken the Red Army into Berlin, firmly stood to attention: sing hup fol-de-rol la la!

8

A SWEDISH SUFFRAGETTE

Unfree. This word is probably the best one to describe the life of a Swedish woman during the nineteenth century: locked up under a father's, brother's or husband's guardianship, without the opportunity of higher education, without the right to inherit on the same terms as a man or to take care of her own income.

Fredrika Bremer partly broke out of that cage and made a path for other women to follow. She was the literary soul sister of Jane Austen, although she was born fifteen years later than Austen and the two never met. Bremer argued for women's rights in at first an unobtrusive way, then a more rebellious one. She became a writer, a worldwide celebrity, and befriended other writers such as H. C. Andersen, Ralph Waldo Emerson, and Henry David Thoreau.

Her mother had three principles for raising children: they were to know as little as possible of the evil of the world, they should be well educated, and they should hardly eat. The purpose of the first principle was to preserve the children's innocent minds. The education they were to receive consisted of language, sewing, music, and drawing. The third principle was enforced because Fredrika Bremer's mother detested 'strong, long and heavily built women'. Girls were supposed to be delicate and petite. Fredrika and her siblings therefore received a small piece of crispbread and a small plate of milk in the morning. Dinner was served at two o'clock and was the happiest time of the day, as they got three small dishes and could eat their fill. At eight o'clock in the evening they again had a glass of cold milk and a piece of crispbread.

The young Fredrika felt less beloved than her siblings and suffered from not being considered graceful. Qualities of charm and beauty were held in high regard at the Bremer home and her mother never stopped reminding her of what she, Fredrika, lacked.

At the age of twenty, she became aware of the injustices perpetrated on women in society and felt strongly that it was wrong for Christianity to confirm them. On the contrary, the true Christian approach would be to view God's creations — woman as well as man — as of equal value. As for the daily life of an upper-middle-class woman, it was a prison built of dullness and enforced passivity.

'How quietly, like muddy water, time stands for a maiden,

who, during a boring and idle life, drags out her days,' she wrote.[8]

According to Swedish law, all unmarried women were minors under the guardianship of their closest male relative until they married (and were then placed under the guardianship of their husbands). When their father died, Fredrika Bremer and her unmarried sister became wards of their elder brother who had complete control over their finances, and who squandered the family fortune over a period of ten years. The only remedy for the situation was to appeal directly to the king; if a woman could prove herself capable and responsible enough, she might be given the blessing of legal majority: Swedish values in 1840.

So, Fredrika Bremer began her lifelong attempt to break out from the cage. At the time, she was already writing novels that were published anonymously. Her *Teckningar utur hvardagslifvet* (*Sketches of Everyday Life*) became an immediate success; in retrospect, it is considered the first realist novel in Sweden, based as it was on an everyday way of talking and authentic details. Her books became extremely popular. When her real identity was revealed, she was awarded a gold medal by the Royal Swedish Academy.

Her theme, recognisable in most of her books, was one of ugly daughters in patriarchal families, women who longed for freedom. In the plot beneath the plot lay the political message of an unmarried woman's fight for the right to legal majority.

8 From Fredrika Bremer's diary, 1 March 1823, currently held by the Swedish National Archives.

The books were translated into several languages. Fredrika Bremer soon became one of the world's most read novelists, wildly popular in Britain and in the US.

When invited to America in 1849, she travelled 'not even accompanied by a chambermaid' and returned to Sweden only two years later. Although she made new friends, like Waldo Emerson and Walt Whitman, who both praised her work, she was disappointed by the American women. They were as much like little geese as the women in Europe, she complained. Nevertheless, the trip left a deep impression. Later, she would compare women's position within society with that of the slaves in America. Out of that anger, the novel *Hertha* was born in 1856.

'How obscure and small is the space you leave for women here on earth!'

In the book, the heroine Hertha is a young woman determined to change society rather than get married and build a family. She would never want a daughter in a world that regarded the birth of a girl with indifference or dissatisfaction. Instead she wishes to 'free her bound sisters'. Hertha fights to introduce day-care centres as well as women's history as a taught subject.

Fredrika Bremer took a huge risk with her new novel. Up until now, she had been a bestselling author who carefully balanced her political ideas by keeping the readers in a good mood.

No more of that. To make sure the message would get through, she even added a postscript concerning the legal progress so far of women's rights in Sweden. The bitter medicine was to be swallowed without honey.

The effect was huge. For two years the debate raged, not only around women's right to independence, but also on the raising of children and creating a society in which women and men contributed on equal terms. Women must be allowed to study to become teachers, doctors, and priests. The women's liberation movement had not yet been initiated, but Fredrika Bremer lay the foundation for what would come. Several men were deeply engaged in the work of improving the legal status and living conditions of women, and many women devoted their lives to accomplish change. The debate caused by *Hertha* only came to an end when a new law was introduced ensuring every woman of twenty-five years of age possessed legal majority. From there it slowly moved onwards.

In 1864, a husband was no longer allowed to beat his wife.

In 1873, women were allowed to study in the universities (although not yet to become priests or lawyers).

In 1874, married women were allowed to handle their income.

In 1884 came a motion for women's right to vote. Declined. It would take another thirty-odd years until Swedish women were allowed to vote. Sweden was the last country in the

Nordic region to recognise women as eligible citizens, in 1919.

As for Fredrika Bremer, she died in 1865 and wouldn't live to see her dreams come true. Swedish women's freedom is now statutory and as great as men's. But would she have been satisfied, she who once wrote: 'What our Swedish unmarried women, both younger and older, still need is freedom, a strong awareness of its value and of their own ability to use it.'

Do women of today use their freedom? Are they aware of their ability to use it? Or does Fredrika Bremer's vision, her words, still need to be realised, embroidered in cross stitches and hung on the wall of every classroom, workplace, in every home, and in every room where unmarried (and married) women spend their lives?

9

KNOW THYSELF

There is something about Skansen, the world's oldest open-air museum, in Stockholm. Inside the gates time moves at a different pace, the hours are stretched into long, almost endless periods, and chronology ceases to exist. Even though the walls to the outside world aren't particularly high, Skansen appears to be a separate space, a world within the world and yet separated from the world at the same time. A parenthesis where multiple layers of time exist simultaneously and therefore there is no actual time at all.

Perhaps that was the plan. The founder, Artur Hazelius, was never really interested in the order of events, but seemed to prefer a geographical principle when placing rune-stones and buildings from the eighteenth century next to each other. Skåne's cultural heritage was laid in the southwest and the Sami cultural heritage in the northwest; in the middle, he'd put

Dalarna. Everything and everybody were welcome at Artur Hazelius' open-air museum — except time. And if time happened to enter, it must be stopped.

Ideas are often inherited from one generation to the next. This was especially true in the Hazelius family. Artur Hazelius' father was an army officer, who founded schools for military education and wrote books about artillery and fortification. His wish was to contribute to Swedish culture, making it richer and more vital. Together with his close friend, the writer Carl Jonas Love Almqvist, he went on long walks, discussing the ideal beauty of the simple country life. He and his friend were also involved in an influential patriotic association, where young men fulfilled 'the spirit of old Sweden'. Thus, the ideals that would lead to the creation of Skansen were introduced to Artur Hazelius at an early age. For his upbringing, his father sent him to different parts of the Swedish countryside in order to get to know the customs and the nature. Artur Hazelius became interested in folk traditions and learned how to weave. To him, the life of a farmer seemed to symbolise everything that was noble and exalted: proximity to the earth and a life in harmony with the divine nature. In Hazelius' vocabulary, it could all be summarised in a single word: Swedishness.

After studying at university and then writing popular nationalist children's books, Artur Hazelius took time out. For two years he did nothing but ask himself what to do with his life. Where could he leave a patriotic mark on the world? Should he become an archaeologist? Should he devote himself to erecting rune stones? Meanwhile his wife had to let some rooms in their home in order to keep the household running.

One thing worried him more than anything else: industrialisation. He couldn't stop thinking about it. During a trip to the landscape of Dalarna he had witnessed the old life disappearing. Nature's beauty was ruined when workshops and industries were built; traditions were exchanged for consumption when the farmers became rich. Everything he knew and loved seemed to change: the way people dressed, what they ate, even how they viewed religion. And that's when he found the purpose of his life. He would save the past from the future. Clothing, furniture, tools, paintings, music, dances, words, traditions, the lot, were to be collected and preserved.

Being a collector as such was not a novelty. The original part of his idea concerned what to collect. Hazelius yearned for stuff which was considered insignificant and common. The ideas planted in him by his father and the writer Almqvist were now fully grown into a life's task.

Artur Hazelius took the motto 'Know thyself' and got down to work. He travelled around Sweden, bought things, and took them to Stockholm; thousands of things, tens of thousands, hundreds of thousands. Soon, he had over a million items in his collection, which became so wild and unsorted that he created a foundation to build a museum where it all could be kept. Nordiska Museet (The Nordic Museum) in Stockholm is the result.

For 25,000 Swedish krona, he bought some land on the Skansenhill next to the museum, and started to build roads, clean ponds, and plant trees. He bought all the land he possibly could, using his own money and donations. He then bought buildings, one from the south of Sweden, another from the western part, a Sami summer residence from the north, and placed them here and there in his open-air museum to be.

The houses would look neatly authentic indoors, but outside no attempt was made to recreate the landscape where they once stood. A parenthesis was created, where he built a world of his own. Friends contributed to the collection during their travels in the country. Hazelius occasionally sent them small sums of money along with detailed instructions for their purchases.

Skansen opened in 1891 and quickly became popular. Particularly enticing were the many festivals that Hazelius invented, like celebrating the national day on 6 June or Saint Lucia's Day on 13 December (the latter a treat still given to every Nobel prize laureate as a part of receiving the prize in Stockholm). Most Swedes believe these to be ancient customs, but they were actually born out of Artur Hazelius' imagination. At a time when the ideal of enlightenment and rationality gave way to the romantic focus on emotions and a general longing for national affinity, he provided a collective identity based on cultural heritage.

His motto, 'Know thyself', was once displayed at the entrance to the temple of Apollo where the oracle in Delphi spoke her advice. Originally, it may have been even older, taken from grave scriptures in ancient Egypt. The words became the motto of Socrates, they were used by Plato, and then reached the Romans who translated them into *Nosce Te Ipsum*. In the seventeenth century, the proverb was used by Thomas Hobbes in *Leviathan*, Carl Linnaeus wrote it in the first edition of *Systema Naturæ*, US President Benjamin Franklin quoted it in 1750, the French author Jean-Jacques Rousseau referred to it — and then there's Artur Hazelius.

Today Skansen is on the very top of the tourist list of Stockholm's attractions. Its web site states: 'At Skansen, you can discover Sweden's history and find out how Swedes once lived according to the changing seasons, through the customs and traditions, work, celebrations and everyday life of times gone by.'

Hazelius wanted the people of Sweden to know themselves through their history. Fair enough. He chose a moment in time, before industrialisation, and called it The Past. He then dressed it in folk costumes and furnished it with looms and haybales. He fabricated traditions and gave Sweden a life it had never had.

And there you have it: Skansen — a living picture book beyond time and space, a fragment of time reborn as a universe.

10

HUMAN BEINGS
ARE TO BE PITIED

'Why were you not as I imagined you?' August Strindberg asked the actress Harriet Bosse in a letter a few years after their divorce.[9]

Harriet Bosse was twenty-three years old when the fifty-one-year-old Strindberg proposed. They married on 6 May 1901, but already two days later they were quarrelling. On 30 May she left him, but returned a few weeks later only to end up arguing again as Strindberg refused to accompany her on their honeymoon to Denmark. She left. He cried.

If you leave, if you have left, I do not know! Leaving, left, without having reconciled me with humanity — or with women!

---

9   Quoted in Meidal, Björn, *God dag, mitt barn!*, Stockholm: Bonnier (2002).

Strindberg followed her to Copenhagen, and, for some moments, harmony was within reach. Then the pain arose again; new outbursts awaited them, as well as fervent fresh reunions in the yellow room in the home they shared in Stockholm. (Strindberg inscribed the code XXX in his diary when they had slept together.)

'Why were you not as I imagined you?' The question is the same for anyone who mourns their love — then, now, and in time to come. The image of the loved one, the fantasies and the yearning, is broken against the actual person. For many, the issue arises while love is still ongoing; in the misunderstandings, the rejections, in the possibility and impossibility of sharing one's life and loneliness with another.

While August Strindberg suffered, twisted and turned his sentiments, the black-eyed and much desired Harriet Bosse came and went and fell pregnant with his child. She left him, she returned, he was happy, he made himself unhappy. He was dreaming. He noted his dreams in his diary. He wrote a dream play.

This was his third marriage and there was something repetitive about it. He might have learned something over the years, and yet he knew even less than before. He noticed his own patterns and positions, and made the observation that everyday life repeated itself. Sadness repeated itself. Yearning repeated itself.

In *A Dream Play* people appear but have no names. Instead

they are called the Officer, the Lawyer, the Postman, the Poet. One is an old man, who has to go back to the classroom and be questioned on the multiplication tables, as if in school, as a lifetime punishment. The Lawyer is constantly quarrelling with his wife about which of them cleans the house, unable to break up. And the Postman — well, when he finally gets the green fishing-tools he has imagined his whole life, he cannot help comparing them with how he had hoped them to be: 'It had to be green, but not that green.'

It is into this world that the god Indra's daughter descends. She listens and seeks to understand human existence, which Strindberg himself summarises in one word, actually the worst word he knew: recurrence.

If Indra's daughter wants to understand what it means to be human, she must experience the painful returning of memories, she must undergo 'Repetition-recurrence. To retrace one's own tracks; to be sent back to the task once finished.' The conclusion she draws has become one of Strindberg's most quoted phrases: 'Human beings are to be pitied'.

The sentence shouldn't be interpreted as self-pity, although that was certainly a feeling with which Strindberg was familiar. Instead it should be seen as an expression of a forgiving tenderness, the kind that acknowledges one's shortcomings but still persists. Some of us seek that compassion in love, others in a higher power, mercy.

Nowadays Strindberg's words are quoted both casually and seriously, often with a cheeky smile as a way to accept a peculiar world and an unfair life. They are said as a joke, as a sarcastic comment on a bad film, a lousy dinner, or a sleepless night. They linger on. As he himself once said, 'I'm a hell of a man, capable of many great things.'

11

THE SWEDE THAT INSPIRED HITLER

Of all the possible ways to argue for the rights of one country to rule another, the Swedish political scientist Rudolf Kjellén's line of argument is as vile as it is persistent.

It begins with the Treaty of Kiel, concluded between Britain and Sweden on one side and Denmark and Norway on the other, in 1814. The treaty was among those intended to end the Napoleonic Wars, and it stated that defeated Denmark must hand over Norway to Sweden as the price for peace. The Norwegians refused to comply, rebelled, and even proclaimed independence and adopted a constitution on 17 May 1814 demanding self-government, so Sweden went to war to suppress its neighbour and, after several bloody attacks, Norway gave up. As a Swedish politician at the time put it:

'The Norwegians should not be entreated but ruled with strong thongs and whips.'

Not surprisingly, the involuntary union didn't work. In 1905 it was dissolved — and that is where the man who inspired Hitler found his grounds.

The Swedish political scientist Rudolf Kjellén hated democracy, detested liberalism, and loathed parliamentarism. He had no doubt in his mind that Norway belonged to Sweden, but there was this slight problem of the new Norwegian constitution. It was based on Montesquieu's division of power between three independent spheres: government, parliament, and judiciary — bad ideas, according to Kjellén. Norway must chuck them away and adopt a non-democratic constitution in order to be reunited with Sweden. If not, he feared that the Swedish system would be infected with the highly contagious democratic virus.

Rudolf Kjellén was deeply influenced by the British philosopher Herbert Spencer's theory of the survival of the fittest. He transmitted the concept to whole nations. From his point of view, a nation wasn't the result of its legal systems and the structure of power, but an organic entity.

The conflict with Norway had fuelled his political development. As much as he hated the liberal ideas in Norway, he reluctantly admired the country's strong left-wing nationalism and wanted to promote an equally aggressive nationalism in

Sweden, although conservative. Nationalism constituted the basic element of his theories, which he developed into a worldview, covering every aspect of reality. His view of culture, morality, democracy, parliamentarism, economics, and social affairs was entirely determined by his desire to promote the nation's development of power, no matter what.

In 1914, he wrote the book that would change history. In *Staten som lifsform (The State as a Lifeform)*, he describes the nation as an organic entity, involved in a ruthless struggle for existence and ruled by blind, animal, and amoral drives. War was of necessity. From the depths of the people, a leader would step forward to realise the true will of the masses. The goal was autocracy; the people everything, the individual nothing.

Kjellén had also been a disciple of the German geographer Friedrich Ratzel, the man who coined the term 'Lebensraum'. Now, the Swede continued Ratzel's line of thought and developed something he named 'geopolitics' — the state as a geographic organism. Based on a state's population, its geographical location, and its financial resources, it was fighting with other states for its living space and survival. The country with the best conditions must be allowed to expand into the others.

Enter Karl Haushofer, a German military and academic, leader of the troops on the Western Front during the First World War.

When Kjellén's books became popular in Germany, Karl Haush-ofer was deeply taken with them. What the Swede wrote was everything he himself had thought, though better and more profound.

After the war, Haushofer became a professor of political geography at the University of Munich. There, one of his students became a favourite — his name was Rudolf Hess. And then a new course of events began.

In 1923, Adolf Hitler and the National Socialist German Workers' Party tried to implement a coup d'état. It failed, and Hitler was sentenced to five years in prison for treason. With him was his friend Rudolf Hess, convicted for the same crime. (Actually, they were behind bars for only eight months.) The two were detained together at Landsberg Prison, where they were visited by Hess' mentor — surprise! — Professor Klaus Haushofer.

In 1924, Haushofer travelled to the prison every Wednesday for five months. There, he read aloud from, and lectured about, Rudolf Kjellén's geopolitical theories as well as the concept of Lebensraum, and it all went straight into the book that Adolf Hitler at the time dictated for Rudolf Hess, *Mein Kampf.*[10]

---

10 Herwig, Holger H., *The Demon of Geopolitics*, Lanham: Rowman & Littlefield Publishers (2016).

The concept of geopolitics is to be found still all over the world, and its most aggressive current advocate is probably the Russian political scientist Alexander Dugin (who enjoys the nickname Putin's Rasputin). Anyone seeking to understand our landscape of Brexit, Trump's victory, and the global surge of the far right should read Dugin, at least according to *The Guardian* in 2016.[11] While the Swedish political scientist Rudolf Kjellén died 1922, his geopolitical way of measuring the world lives on.

11 d'Ancona, Matthew, 'Putin and Trump could be on the same side in this troubling new world order', *The Guardian*, 19 December 2016 https://www.theguardian.com/world/commentisfree/2016/dec/19/trump-putin-same-side-new-world-order

12

THE PRESERVATION
OF THE SWEDISH RACE

We are fortunate enough to be of a race that is still quite
pristine, a breed that is a bearer of very high and very
good qualities. It is peculiar that while we are indeed
committed to construct pedigrees for our dogs and
horses, we are not as eager to assure the preservation
of our own Swedish folk stock.

These words were uttered in the Swedish Parliament in 1921,
by a Social Democratic minister-to-be, in an attempt to per-
suade the other members of Parliament to vote in favour of
the founding of a State Institute for Racial Biology. His line of
argument prevailed. Hence Sweden became the first nation in
the world with racial research financed by the state. His words,

and the Swedish values they revealed, kept influencing one decision after the other.

In 1922, the Social Democratic Party suggested that people with mental disorders should be sterilised. The reason was 'the eugenic strain caused by the breeding of the feeble-minded'. While the leader of the Social Democrats signed the bill, there were other party members who opposed it. One of them is quoted as saying: 'You will not stop here, you will go on and sterilise other patients. And then what? What will prevent you from eventually killing them?'

For a number of reasons, that particular bill never became law.

In 1933, Adolf Hitler took power in Germany. One of the first decrees he issued was to order the forced sterilisation of 'the feeble-minded', as well as the congenitally blind and deaf. In connection with work on a similar bill, the then Swedish Minister of Justice, Karl Schlyter, asked his officials to keep an eye on Germany. One might learn something there. Two years later, in 1935, a Swedish law of mass sterilisation was duly passed. 'Feeble-minded' and 'sub-normal' people, disabled people or those living an 'un-social' life, in other words, those who could be expected to become 'a burden to themselves and others' were to be surgically managed.

The reasons for sterilisation were officially threefold: hygienic, social, and medical — and the overall purpose was 'the rehabilitation of the Swedish people, in order to prohibit the perpetuation of the inherited weakness leading to some future individuals who are not desirable members of a healthy society'.

Between 1928 and 1976, approximately 63,000 Swedish citizens were subjected to sterilisation. During the same period, 58,000 Finnish citizens were sterilised. The same goes for 41,000 Norwegians and 11,000 Danes.

How come the Nordic countries became world-leaders in sterilisation with Sweden top of the class?

One explanation lies within the core of those words uttered in the Swedish parliament in 1921, the idea of an 'unspoiled race' with 'very high and very good qualities'. They hint at a general notion of the existence of a hierarchy of human 'races' whose superior strains should be kept pure and not diluted by bad genes.

Another reason is Martin Luther and his Reformation. All the European nations which passed laws of mass sterilisation were Protestant. The Catholic countries were opponents of the concept for the same reason they are against contraceptives and abortion: what God has created should not be interfered with by humankind. What is holier than conception?

But there is also a third reason why the Nordic countries specifically proved so inclined to sterilise their own population: the welfare system.

In all times, people have deviated from the norm, become ill, or needed help. But the idea of sterilising them does not arise until society begins to weld together by common welfare. As soon as welfare is based on all citizens contributing — through diligence, work, and a subsequent high tax — those who are not considered contributors become a problem. It is no coincidence that all the Nordic countries put forward similar legislation within the same decade. It was about securing the majority's wellbeing at the expense of a few. By stopping women who were considered weak or unstable from having children, the state could preserve the 'race' as well as prevent unmarried mothers from becoming a burden to society.

In fact, when General Child Support was introduced in Sweden in 1948, some of the leading social welfare engineers were worried that the state support would encourage 'genetical poorer elements' to breed. Several authorities demanded that the reform should be accompanied by increased opportunities for sterilisation. Their appeals were not unheard. The year before child support was introduced, over two thousand people were sterilised; six people a day — a new Swedish record.

The operation was supposed to be voluntary, but refusing was seldom an option. Often, the procedure was suggested to young women who had become pregnant without being married. They were allowed an abortion on condition that they also underwent sterilisation. Or they were imprisoned in a correctional institution of sorts because of 'unsocial' behaviour (often a euphemism for sexual activity), but would be set free if they agreed to be sterilised. Over 90 per cent of those operated on were women.[12]

In the ideal community, where all citizens are expected to be healthy, hard working, and tax paying, those who failed to meet expectations have to be excluded. The logic of 'racial hygiene' merged with the economic fundamentals of the welfare society.

Sweden's position at the top of the league for performing sterilisation on its own citizens at this time is attributable also to some additional factors. There was no system of private health care, practically all doctors were employed by the state. In England and France for instance, where the majority of doctors had their own practice, there were no laws concerning operations of mass sterilisation — there would simply not be anyone obliged to perform them.

Today, some 1,600 people in Sweden have received state compensation for the forced sterilization they went through — all in all 175,000 Swedish kronor, the equivalent of £17,500 each.

---

12   Palmblad, Eva, 'Abortpolitikens dolda dagordning under 30- och 40-talen. Fem uppsatser om steriliseringen i Sverige', *Lund Studies in the History of Science and Ideas*, Gothenburg: University of Gothenburg (2000).

13

THE PEOPLES' HOME

There is no way of understanding the core of the Swedish self-image without understanding the word 'folkhem', which literally translates as 'peoples' home'. Its origins lie in a kind of self-help establishment in Germany, the 'Volksheim', established in the growing industrial cities around the turn of the twentieth century. There, workers could read books and newspapers, listen to lectures, and eat a bowl of soup.

How come the 'folkhem' became the prime symbol for Sweden in the twentieth century? Can the concept be defined — or is it conveniently unprecise, possible to fill with whatever meaning one considers suitable? Whatever the case, the word itself and the underlying, albeit diffuse, idea is strongly associated with the social democratic vision that shaped Sweden into a welfare state.

It was a bumpy road. In the years preceding the First World

War, when nationalism swept over Europe like a malign fever, the Social Democrats talked about the shared goals of the workers of the world and ended all their meetings by singing 'The Internationale'. The conservatives took every chance to accuse them of being un-patriotic — un-Swedish — and even pacifistic. Such grave allegations had to be fought, and somewhere in the process the concept of 'folkhem' appeared as an answer to the problem.

The Swedish leader of the Social Democratic party and future prime minister, Per Albin Hansson, had mentioned the 'folkhem' now and then during the 1920s, but it was during a speech in Parliament in 1928 that the concept surfaced, was criticised by the opposition, and then debated in the press — in short, became politics.

The word 'folk' originates from the German word for people, 'volk', which trended during the Nazi era in slogans like *Volk ohne raum* (A people without room) or *Ein Volk, ein Reich, ein Führer* (One people, one country, one leader) — not to mention the Volkswagen.

But 'the people' was not a social democratic concept — on the contrary. If one speaks of people, one does not speak about class or of economic and social diversity. The word 'folk' hides the traditional leftish analysis under a nationalistic fog. But Per Albin Hansson was a clever man. He introduced the 'folkhem' concept in order to gain ground from the nationalistic conservative and anti-democratic parts of society. He wanted to build a home for the Swedish people, a folk-home:

> A home is based on a sense of togetherness and belonging. The good home does not know any privilege or disadvantage, no favourites or stepchildren. There, one does not look down upon the other, nor is one trying to profit from the other, the strong do not seek to oppress the weak and plunder them. In the good home there is equality, consideration, cooperation, helpfulness. Applied to the folkhem, this would mean breaking the social and economic barriers that now separate citizens from each other and divide them into privileged and underprivileged, into ruling and ruled, wealthy and impoverished, robber and robbed.

Per Albin Hansson simply took the concept of the national right and filled it with leftist substance. The merger becomes a vitally important factor in the victory of the Social Democrats in their first election in 1932.

While Hitler was taking power in Germany the following year, the Swedish Prime Minister was able to integrate the central Nazi concept of nationalism into a Social Democrat theory of equality:

Democracy and the peoples' community are the words of today. They are often understood as opposites, but in order to make any sense they must mean the same. A democracy of today strives to realise the people's feelings of national solidarity, and an actual peoples' community can only appear when there exist equal rights, opportunities, and obligations for all.

He launched a series of measures in order to deal with unemployment and was heavily criticised because he chose to cooperate with one of the conservative parties in doing so. But the Swedish Social Democrats wanted to learn their German lesson. The recent victory of the Nazis had clearly shown that by far the most dangerous threat to democracy was a high rate of unemployment. The passivity of German social democracy, its inability to deal with the unemployment problem: this was considered one of the main reasons for Hitler's success.

Observing German Social Democrats standing helpless before the overwhelming success of the Nazi Party, Per Albin Hansson appropriated the nationalistic weapon and turned it into a social democratic tool: the idea of Sweden as a peoples' community. Social justice was one main component. Another was promoting the idea of a mythical people with a common soul of sorts as a way of unifying a new society based on material welfare and in need of emotional ties between people living there.

The German Social Democrats had left the idea of the nation untouched, free to be exploited by the anti-democrats. Per Albin Hansson was not about to make the same mistake. The Swedish people must be made aware that there was nothing that the Nazis in Germany could achieve with dictatorship that the Social Democrats could not achieve in Sweden with democracy. It worked. Per Albin Hansson's rhetorical coup laid the foundation for something unique in the world's political history: forty-four unbroken years of social democratic government, between the 1930s and the 1970s.

14

TAKE OFF YOUR SHOES

I admit that I have thought of Sweden as a 'country of peasants', with a slight disdain inherited from my immigrant parents. They grew up in two of Europe's oldest metropolises, one in London and the other in Budapest, and met in Sweden in the 1960s.

In my childhood home in our not-so-posh Stockholm suburb, there was frequent talk about Swedish values. For instance, the fact that people who invited you to dinner expected their guests to take their shoes off, something quite incomprehensible for my parents. To dress up and then spend the evening barefoot?

For me, it was a matter of adapting my families' values to those of the country in which I was born. I soon realised the possible insult that lay in keeping your shoes on indoors, as well as that of bringing indoor shoes with you on visits, which prompted much bourgeois snobbery, especially in the 1970s.

Not an option. For my parents, it never became a major problem as they mostly partied with British, American, and Hungarian friends, people who never considered socialising in their socks. For them, this unwritten law was simply a legacy from the days when all Swedes were farmers coming home with dirty boots from working their acres of clay all day. But they were mistaken.

The original problem had actually been the opposite, that people in Sweden had not taken their shoes off when coming home. Dirt and bacteria had been allowed into kitchens and bedrooms, where people lived all crammed up together. Then came the 1930s and the pursuit of modernity. Light, health, and purity became vital concepts, and to implement change in society, the home and housing played a crucial role. As two of the main engineers of the Swedish welfare system, the couple Alva and Gunnar Myrdal, wrote in 1934:

> Healthy and adequate housing for everyone is the essential prerequisite for physical and spiritual health. Unless this prerequisite is met, all our efforts to raise our people's standard intellectually and morally, socially as well as economically, will become largely futile. Housing policy is therefore a basic requirement for all prophylactic social policies, in the overall endeavour to increase the quality of the population.

For the first time ever, the Swedish state financed housing; the building of 12,000 apartments especially meant for families with scarce economic resources was initiated. Consequently, the tenants had to be educated not to bring old habits into brand-new homes. Those who failed could be evicted. As the Myrdal couple put it: monitoring must become efficient. Hence, rules for home inspection were tightened in the 1936 Health Care Standards. Home inspectors — yes, that's right — should act as controllers on behalf of society, and their mission included more than checking the degree of damp or cold. In the home inspector's instructions, the cleanliness of the homes was emphasised. People mustn't 'unnecessarily' make a mess. A door mat or similar cleaning device for footwear must be provided. One must not spit on the floor — a filthy habit according to the Medical Board, and furthermore a health hazard to crawling infants. Rubbish should be carried out as soon as possible, and the smaller the home, the greater importance of keeping it clean.

The people living in the home must also keep clean to avoid unpleasant smells. Everyone should 'be subjected to thorough cleaning' at least once a week. Ventilation by opening several windows should be arranged in connection with making the beds, after cooking, and before bedtime. In Stockholm, the inspectors spread information leaflets to the households. Each family must understand that the quality of the accommodation was not a private matter, but something that concerned society as a whole. Last but not least, the inspectors must ensure that people took their shoes off.

A Swedish value created by a state order. I'm quite happy my parents never obeyed.

15

PERSONAL IDENTIFICATION
NUMBERS

The most chameleon-coloured word in the Swedish language is 'personnummer' (personal identification numbers). It invisibly adapts to its surroundings. Most Swedes can say their own number in their sleep. In fact, they mumble them several times a day — so plain, so common, and so anonymous, and yet so profoundly significant.

If anyone came up with the idea of writing a book about the year of 1947, the introduction then of personal identification numbers in Sweden ought to be included as a time marker. On the other hand, there was such a long-standing centralising tendency behind them that the actual introduction didn't represent a sudden change of national mood, but simply a natural consequence of how Swedish society was organised according to the wishes of a few powerful men.

The structure of the Swedish state is the result of the relentless warfare conducted by King Gustav II Adolf combined with the organising skills and orderly mind of his chancellor Axel Oxenstierna. Both were phenomena born out of the rule of old Gustav Vasa, often named the father of modern Sweden. He did something unusual in the sixteenth-century Europe of small principalities and feudal lords: he centralised power.

While other contemporary rulers left the managing of their provinces to local lords, Gustav Vasa placed loyal bailiffs all around the country to take charge of law and order. The bailiffs became intermediaries between the nation's inhabitants and the king himself and thus gave Gustav Vasa full control of communication with his people. (Today he would have used Twitter.)

The bailiffs' main task was to mobilise support for the rule of Gustav Vasa while keeping an eye on his political opponents. In addition, they provided him with direct information about the kingdom's resources in the form of buildings, livestock, and mills, all of it conveniently taxable. In other words, the availability of levers for controlling the population, economy, and trade increased. Three times the peasants rebelled against the king's excessive controls and high taxes. Each time he pushed them back using brutal methods and tightened his grip on the Swedish population even more. Once Gustav Vasa introduced hereditary succession to the throne, his sons would continue his way of ruling, and so would his grandson, King Gustav II Adolf.

It is the latter who appointed the Lord High Chancellor Axel Oxenstierna in 1612, at a time when the condition of the kingdom could be described as a medieval mess. There was a lot to be done, and luckily the Lord High Chancellor Oxenstierna had forty-two years in this post to do it.

Sweden without Axel Oxenstierna would have been another country, hard to imagine. He established order in the justice system as well as in the postal system. He suggested that every city should have a bank. He persuaded Gustav II Adolf to donate a fortune to Uppsala University, with seventeen new professors as a result; he contributed his own resources in order to establish several schools; and so on. His main driving force was King Gustav II Adolf's seemingly endless need for soldiers and cash. Thirty years of warfare tends to empty the vaults.

Once a year, all men over fifteen years of age were required to stand in rows outside the village church in order for the bailiffs to inspect them. One out of ten was then sent to be a soldier. It didn't take long for people to realise that half of them would be dead within a year due to diseases like typhus, so they failed to appear for inspection. This had to be taken care of and Lord High Chancellor Axel Oxenstierna was the man to do it.

He turned to the parishes and checked the books where the members of the congregation were recorded in connection with baptism and burial, and thus he knew all he needed to keep track of every fifteen-year-old male in Sweden.

One thing led to another. The King needed soldiers and the soldiers needed pay. In order for that to happen, taxes had to be increased. In order to collect them, one needed bailiffs, and in order to increase their number, one had to build schools to educate them in their profession. In connection with these schools, new cities appeared: a nation in the making.

The Lord High Chancellor Oxenstierna went on to create a hierarchical state apparatus where lower levels reported to higher. Controls were introduced to increase the quality of management through example, correction, and instruction. Matters were to be dealt with expertly and without delay — ideals that are still enshrined in today's regulations and policies.

The expanding control of the population mounted up to the point in 1947 when all residents received a number consisting of nine numbers: the individual's birth date plus a three-digit number. Twenty years later, a check digit was added for security reasons.

Today, a Swede cannot be born, educated, marry, divorce, become ill, or die without a personal identification number. It has become such a casual act to declare one's individual set of digits, even to collect bonus points in connection with purchases in department stores, that many simply say them loud and clear in any given situation. Most of Sweden's inhabitants are entered by their numbers in hundreds of registers of various kinds, and every government and municipal activity is based on the use of the residents' personal identification numbers. It's almost an equation of Orwellian design: a centralised state plus digitisation plus a growing private market of health care and similar services, turns the personal identification number into a key that opens every aspect of a human life.

In many countries, also within the EU, residents are obliged to carry identity documents — they must always be able to prove who they are. In Sweden there is no such law. And this is where a specific Swedish paradox appears: the citizen is free from this obligation if she can prove that she is a Swedish citizen, which is done by providing a valid identity document or revealing her personal identification number.

16

IKEA

I once met Ingvar Kamprad, the Ikea founder. It was in August 2010 at Ikea's head office, in the small town of Almhult, Sweden. (The address is 1 Ikea Street.) I was writing a book about his closest friend, Otto Ullman — a Jewish refugee from Austria hired as a farmhand by the Kamprad family during the war — and had asked for a meeting. Once we'd introduced ourselves, Mr Kamprad took hold of me by the waist, as if we were on the dance floor and he wanted to check out my figure. Then we sat down, my recorder went on, and an interview of two and a half hours began.[13]

It is hard to overstate the size of Mr Kamprad's empire. Stepping off the train at the Almhult station, you have two pedestrian bridges to choose from: one takes you into the

---

13 I used this as the basis for my book on Ingvar Kamprad, *And in the Vienna Woods the Trees Remain*. Translated by Saskia Vogel. New York: Other Press (2020).

town itself, with a population of around 10,000; the other takes you to Ikea — or, to be more precise, to the Ikea Hotel, Ikea Tillsammans (a cultural centre), the Ikea Museum, and the Ikea Test Lab, along with a sprawling complex of corporate departments. And while most of the world knows Ikea solely for its inexpensive furniture and giant blue stores, in Sweden its image is inextricable from the life of Ingvar Kamprad. In the museum, design history intermingles with family snapshots.

As with the bridges at Almhult, there are also two ways into the Ikea story. One is uplifting and inspirational: a young man from a modest background, but with more than the usual dose of business acumen, builds an empire. Although the hero of the story makes the occasional mistake, that is precisely what makes him human and such a treasured symbol of Swedishness.

The other way leads from Mr Kamprad's childhood and adolescence in a Hitler-loving family, Germans who had immigrated from the Sudetenland, in Czechoslovakia, where both his paternal grandmother and his father were Nazis; his long-lasting commitment to the Swedish fascist movement; and his membership, during the Second World War, of Sweden's Nazi party, Swedish Socialist Unity. Both stories are equally true.

The 1990s brought two major news reports pointing to Mr Kamprad's involvement in the Swedish Nazi party and his lasting affinity for Per Engdahl, who led the country's anti-Semitic fascist movement after the war. The articles attracted attention at the time, but the whole thing blew over quickly. So strong was the Ikea brand that nothing seemed able to affect it.

But after my interview with Mr Kamprad, I continued to investigate — and there proved to be more. In the Swedish Security Service's archive, I found his file from 1943, labelled 'Memorandum concerning: Nazi' and stamped 'secret' in red letters.

Ingvar Kamprad, then seventeen years old, was Member No. 4,014 of Swedish Socialist Unity, the country's leading far-right party during the war. Sweden's general security service had apparently kept him under surveillance for at least eight months, confiscating and reading his correspondence.

In November 1942, he wrote that he had recruited 'quite a few comrades' to the party and missed no opportunity to work for the movement. The memorandum about his correspondence reached the Sixth Division of the Stockholm police on 6 July 1943. Six days later, Mr Kamprad sent an application to the county administrative office in Vaxjo to register his new company, Ikea.

When did Kamprad leave the Swedish Nazi Party? No one has so far managed to find out the answer to that question. On the other hand, we know that his involvement in Per Engdahl's fascist organisation, the New Swedish Movement, continued after the end of the war. He invited comrades from the movement to his home in Elmtaryd and was regarded as their benefactor. There are letters where he is asked to donate or thanked for the latest contribution. Kamprad also acted as publisher for one of the fascist leader Per Engdahl's books. The two had become close friends and called each other 'BB': best brother. Engdahl was invited to Kamprad's first wedding in 1951, a quiet affair in a church outside Stockholm, at which he gave a beautiful speech.

During the first two years after the war, Per Engdahl received refugees, hid them from their persecutors, and helped transport them to safety — Nazi refugees, that is. By 1945, Engdahl had created a network for Europe's shattered Nazi and fascist movements, as he was afraid the ideas would die with them. His underground network interlinked Oswald Mosley's blackshirts, Belgian Flams Bloc, Dutch Nazis, French fascists, Germans who were still loyal to Hitler, Swiss hardcore Nazis, remnants of the Hungarian Arrow Cross movement, the Italian MSI, who propagated Benito Mussolini's ideas, as well as Danish and Norwegian Nazis. They were all there. In 1951, the secret network became official as the participants gathered in the Swedish town Malmö where they, under Engdahl's leadership, established the 'Malmö Movement' (also called ESB, the Europäische Soziale Bewegung, or European Social Movement).

A magazine, *Nation Europe*, was started in order to give the 'Malmö Movement' a platform and a voice. There, the genocide of the Jews was denied and the idea of an un-democratic, white Europe was promoted. Per Engdahl was part of the editorial board. His book, *Västerlandets förnyelse* (*The Renewal of the West*), became the movement's official book.

What could Ingvar Kamprad have known, what did he support? Nobody can really say for sure. All that is certain is that during these crucial years, he and Per Engdahl were friends and kept in touch. In late autumn 1951, Ingvar wrote a letter to Per Engdahl, to thank him for his book, *The Renewal of the West*. From time to time, Per Engdahl came to visit. Once he bought a sofa from Ingvar Kamprad and his Ikea, but it is unclear if he got a discount.

The company Ikea was innovative in several ways. Being able to see the goods in a catalogue before buying them was an entirely new phenomenon. Shopping in a kind of warehouse outside the city centre had not been done before, but motoring and a new lifestyle prioritising consumption made it possible to suggest the department store as a weekend outing.

In 1955, Ikea started to sell furniture of its own design. Ten years later, when Ikea opened in Stockholm, thousands of people queued outside. The timing was brilliant. The huge new 48,000-square metre department store went up just beside a motorway going through newly built suburbs where tens of thousands families needed to furnish their homes without having a lot of money spare to do so. There was also a restaurant serving meatballs. Ikea began to be associated with 'Swedishness'.

In 1973, the first shop outside Scandinavia was established, in Switzerland. The expansion meant that the company became an ambassador for Sweden abroad. Swedish names on the furniture and the staff wearing the so-called 'Ikea Costume', which consisted of jeans, shirt, and jumper, helped to promote the idea of Sweden as down-to-earth-exotic and trendy at the same time.

In the immediate postwar years, people weren't interested in revisiting their Nazi or fascist past; maybe they still aren't. Mr Kamprad has come to symbolise the driven Swedish entrepreneur, the artful trend spotter, the strong, enthusiastic leader — the man who gives the consuming masses what the masses yearn for. He is a role model as well as a reflection of the Swedish image. Ikea markets Sweden, which in its turn markets Ikea, and so nation and company become images of each other, while their respective self-images expand.

When I published my book containing the new information I'd discovered about Mr Kamprad and his Jewish friend in 2011, news organisations around the world picked up the story. It took a month for Ikea to respond, and when it did it was by way of a $51 million donation to the United Nations High Commissioner on Refugees, the single-largest donation in the agency's history. The bad news paled in the light of this huge gift.

Sweden still hasn't answered the question: who was Ingvar Kamprad? How could he remain loyal to the fascist leader and

Holocaust denier Per Engdahl, belong to a Nazi party and, at the same time, be so fond of his Jewish friend, Otto Ullman? Otto, whose parents were murdered in Auschwitz?

When I repeatedly asked Mr Kamprad for an answer in my interview with him in 2010, I finally received a shocking reply: 'There's no contradiction as far as I'm concerned. Per Engdahl was a great man, and I'll maintain that as long as I live.'

Since my interview, neither I nor any other journalist has had the opportunity to ask about Mr Kamprad's membership of Socialist Unity or his tribute to Engdahl. And now, with his death in January 2018, no one ever will. The Ikea museum mentions that Ingvar's grandmother was very close to her grandson, and that she saw Hitler as Germany's future. That is all.

Ingvar Kamprad's image and Sweden's continue to reflect each other: without shadows, without disgrace, and without any ambition to come to terms with their past.

17

SWEDISH NEUTRALITY

Two concepts significant for the image of Sweden within itself, as well as in the outside world, are neutrality and freedom of alliance. Neutrality, as in not choosing sides when two (or more) states are at war or in dispute; freedom of alliance, as in not tying knots of solidarity to other states. It's generally stated that Sweden has kept up a policy of neutrality and freedom of alliances since the early nineteenth century. It is an interesting lie.

Already around the time of the 1850s Sweden broke the policy after solemnly promising Denmark that it would support it in defending its borders against Prussia. That particular pledge altered Denmark's policies towards Prussia, but when the going got tough the Swedish king withdrew the commitment which, according to Swedish neutrality, never should have been given (and Denmark was then defeated in a humiliating way).

Actually, the whole neutrality issue started with King Gustav IV Adolf — a strange man with a strange life. After his father, King Gustav III, was murdered at the Stockholm Opera, he closed it. After being criticised in a French newspaper, he closed Sweden to the French press and French books. He detested France in general, and Napoleon in particular. As a result, he took Sweden to war against the French Emperor in 1805. No one supported the idea. When Napoleon formed an alliance with Russia, the crisis bloomed into full catastrophe as far as Sweden was concerned. King Gustav IV Adolf refused to accept any peace deals and ended up in a war with France, Denmark, and Russia at the same time. At that point, the king was violently over-thrown by officers of his own army. Nevertheless, the defeat was unavoidable and at the peace agreement in 1809, Sweden lost one third of its territory and one million of its inhabitants. The sorrow and indignation of the Swedish nationalists was bottomless. Finland, which had been a part of Sweden for more than six hundred years, became Russian territory, and Sweden's borders were redrawn and took the shape they still have today.

'As Heaven is my witness, I would have preferred to have signed my own death warrant than this peace treaty,' said Swedish diplomat Curt von Stedingk, who took part in the negotiations.

Now, two lessons were to be learned. Sweden would never again interfere in other countries' wars. Swedish soldiers would never again be sent out to die on foreign battlefields. From then on, Sweden would be neutral. And, even though the country thereafter acted contrary to its own policy of neutrality several times during the nineteenth century, the idea of the neutral country remained at the very core of Swedes' self-image.

The first major breech came at a time when Sweden was torn between the old class-based structure and strong liberal winds of change. In 1914, Sweden was led by a government that wanted to take moves in a democratic direction. The liberal Prime Minister Karl Staaff was in favour of universal suffrage and preferred social reforms to spending money on the country's defences. The conservative nationalists could stand neither him nor his democratic ideas. With the Swedish Queen Victoria in the lead, they fought all attempts to introduce parliamentarism and instead promoted the idea of joining forces with Germany in the event of a war. They loved Germany, but feared Russia. Sweden was considered the 'last country of westerners' and its men were needed to guard the European continent from the Slavic people of the East. It was all about taking back 'our' Finland, honouring the 'bloodlines' to Germany, and reviving the superpower status Sweden had once enjoyed.

The liberal Prime Minister, with his voting rights reform and his ideas of not belonging to any power block, was considered a weak man. He was spat on while he took his morning walk through the fashionable parts of Stockholm on his way to the Parliament, he was called a traitor, and there were ashtrays decorated with his face where one could put out a cigar.

The conservative movement organised a march where 30,000 farmers protested against disarmament, and they were received by the Swedish king on the castle's courtyard. The king's speech was a direct attempt to discredit the prime minister and dissolve the Swedish government — and it was a success. The government was forced to resign. When the First World War broke out, the conservatives were euphoric and, without hesitating, stood on Germany's side against Russia. No neutrality. No freedom of alliance.

'Our preparedness is good', Prime Minister Per Albin Hansson said in August 1939. That was not true. When the Second World War broke out, Sweden's defence was weak again and the soldiers lacking in war experience. When Germany invaded Denmark in 1940, the neighbouring southern parts of Sweden were protected only by police patrols and small military forces where each soldier had a limited number of cartridges for his weapon.

As for the neutrality, it only took some Nazi pressure for

the Swedish government to abandon it. In May 1940, German troops were trapped in Narvik, in the north of Norway, and help could only reach them via Swedish railways. Soon, the first major agreement with the Nazis was a fact: soldiers, military equipment, humanitarian aid, and healthcare workers were to be sent through Sweden. And, despite the fact that the Swedish Prime Minister Per Albin Hansson had informed the people that no concessions to Germany would be made as long as the war was continuing, his government allowed even more transits of so-called 'humanitarian character' through the country. (But did anyone really believe that a thousand German soldiers needed a total of four hundred doctors and nurses?) The concessions continued, one transit train after the other, so German soldiers in Norway would get food, weapons, and could go on leave. On 18 June 1940, Prime Minister Hansson wrote in his diary: 'Thus we broke our dear and strictly held neutralism because of our knowledge that it would be unreasonable in the current situation to take the risk of having a war.'

Sweden had already given up its goal of following a policy of strict neutrality, in favour of a policy aimed at keeping the country out of war. In order to protect Sweden against a possible German attack, iron ore mines were packed with explosives. If Sweden was occupied, the valuable natural resource, crucial to the Germans' war effort, could be blasted into smithereens.

Was there a real threat of Germany occupying Sweden

— would that have been the result if Sweden hadn't conceded to Hitler's wishes? Probably not. New German research has shown that no actual German plans to attack Sweden were made, nor were there military resources for carrying out any assault. But how could Prime Minister Hansson be sure?

From July 1940 to November 1941, a total of 686,000 German soldiers travelled by train through Sweden, up to 1,400 men a day. Every week, wagons with 'goods' were transported to Nazi positions in Norway and Finland — a total of 5,000 wagons. Approximately half of the goods were considered to be war material.

Through Swedish waters there were twenty-six German shipments on more than seventy vessels. In addition, Nazi Germany had permission to send circa sixty courier flights a week between Germany, Norway, and Finland. This was probably more a question of passenger traffic than courier or mail traffic. In the northern town Luleå, the Germans had established a large warehouse of goods that was driven to Finland by Swedish lorries. The Swedish army also provided around 4,000 German soldiers with tents and stoves.

Throughout the war, Germany was one of Sweden's most important trading partners, providing Sweden with coal and charcoal in order to heat people's houses, and keep the factories going and the trains working throughout the winters. In return, Sweden sold Germany iron ore and steel.

The Swedish government balanced on a thin moral dividing line. Britain and the Allies become irritated with the Swedish-German trade, but Sweden also needed British oil and undertook an extensive trade in wood with both England and the United States. The strategy was to pretend that exports to Germany were within the 'normal' quota, although in fact they were significantly increased as a direct consequence of the Nazi rearmament policy. Despite the efforts of the Allies to stop Swedish exports of ball-bearings to Nazi Germany, Sweden maintained its trade with Germany almost throughout the entire war. Only on 12 October 1944 did Sweden ban all further exports of ball-bearings and roller-bearings to Germany.

Since then, the question has been raised whether this was a good strategy or not. Is it thanks to Prime Minister Hansson that Sweden was kept out of the war? What was the moral cost for keeping the Nazis in a good mood? Did Sweden excel in defending democratic values under pressure? All interesting and important issues, but maybe the crucial question is: if Sweden had acted differently and taken a rather more truly neutral line — could the war have had another course, ended sooner even?

During the Cold War that followed, the Swedish neutrality doctrine was summarised in the formula 'Freedom of alliance in peace, with the purpose of neutrality in war'. The message to the outside world was that if war came, Sweden would not be taking sides.

After the end of the Cold War, the wording changed once again. Now it stated 'Sweden's military freedom of alliance, aimed at neutralising our country in the event of war in our immediate area remains'. In case of war, Sweden would choose whatever best protected national security in the specific situation. It might be neutral or it might not.

Below the surface, Sweden had become closely linked to the United States through cooperation agreements and military cooperation and finally, in the year of 2000, neutrality was completely deleted from the Swedish strategic doctrine. What never was, has now ceased to be, officially.

18

AS THE HAND GRIPS
A SUN-WARM STONE

Stones everywhere.

A lot of people collect stones with a streak of greed, as if each stone grants them ownership of the place where it was picked up. People carry stones in their pockets for no particular reason, as an extra weight, to roll through their fingers during the long wait in a shopping queue or while riding a bus. Stones are placed on windowsills where they collect light and reflect it. Their presence lacks any deeper meaning. They are chosen for their smoothness, their colours, their traces of long-extinct animals, because they glisten, or are matte, because they have a pattern of stripes or because they have no stripes at all, because they exist, the windowsill exists, and so does the light.

When the sun shines on a rock, it accumulates heat. When the ore is heated enough in a blast furnace, iron is extracted and the remainder is glazed to slag. All over Bergslagen, the part of Sweden where iron has been extracted since the twelfth century, one can collect the glass-like slagstones, turquoise or misty green.

The Swedish landscape is a landscape of stones. Rocks have been moved by the ice sheet covering the land 10,000 years ago and have since rolled all over the place, leaving deep scraping traces in the granite, shaping and reshaping the land; stone walls mark borders and stones are erected in order to commemorate.

The Rök Runestone is supposedly the oldest preserved text in Swedish literary history. It's a block of light-grey fine-grain granite, about 382 cm high (of which 125 cm lies below ground) and, with its 760 characters, it has the world's longest runestone inscription, dated back to the early ninth century.

Then there is the so-called Hitler stone. Nazi Germany made major orders of Swedish granite before and during the Second World War, especially from quarries in Blekinge, Skåne, Småland, and Bohuslän. The intention was to build Germania, a new world capital. A lot of granite was subsequently delivered to Germany. In 1943, the transport was stopped due to the war, but the Swedish quarries continued to excavate up until the war ended, storing the stone along the Swedish coasts, and the Germans kept paying punctually. After the war, the blocks of granite remained undelivered to Germany.

In one of his first poems to be published, the Swedish poet and Nobel prize laureate, Tomas Tranströmer, wrote:

In the first hours of day consciousness can embrace the world just as the hand grasps a sun-warm stone.[14]

— a picture of a calm and trustworthy relationship between the self and the world. But even though trust in the world is both a universal experience and a deeply private one — and therefore cannot be narrowed down to being simply Swedish — it is obvious how influenced the poet is by the nature that surrounds him. A sun-warm stone isn't always a good thing.

When the writer Lars Gustafsson taught Tomas Tranströmer's poem to literature students in Austin, Texas, it appeared that sun-warm stones were to be avoided. The heat made them scorching. What is interpreted as an expression of the poet's sense of faith and trust in the universe, the being itself, became something deeply uncomfortable in Texas, even a risk of harm. The differences in both culture and climate provoke varying responses based on the reader's experiences and their body's memories.

Stones, a Swedish value? Why not? After all, in Sweden the word for stone — 'sten' — is even a name.

---

14 Translated by Rika Lesser: https://www.wordswithoutborders.org/article/prelude

19

I AM DEATH

Antonius Block: Who are you?

Death: I'm Death.

Antonius Block: You have come for me?

Death: I've been by your side for a long time.

Stan Marsh's grandfather wants to die. He attempts to take his own life several times but fails, so he talks Stan Marsh into killing him instead. But before this actually happens, Death himself appears, scolding the grandfather. It is not acceptable to coerce one's grandchild — or anyone at all — into killing you. For various reasons, it all ends with Death taking Stan's friend Kenny. Well, for anyone outside the American television series *South Park*'s satirical universe, all this is of course incomprehensible. But that's beside the point. The thing is that when Death appears, he looks like he stepped out of

Ingmar Bergman's film *The Seventh Seal*: the black hood, the black cape, the lot.

Ingmar Bergman supposedly had a strong anxiety about death, which he supposedly cured by returning to the subject again and again, using it in his work. In the 1957 film *The Seventh Seal*, Bergman and the film photographer Gunnar Fischer created something that left its mark on the entire world of popular culture and its way of dealing with death.

Ingmar Bergman often used biblical references and most of his films deal with the meaning and meaninglessness of life as well as with God. The Protestant legacy cannot be ignored. Just as the film makers Robert Bresson, Andrej Tarkovsky, and Lars von Trier were greatly inspired by the Danish film director Carl Theodor Dreyer, so too was Ingmar Bergman. The two also shared the fate of growing up with a father who was a deeply devoted Christian.

Dreyer's scaled-down imagery tends to show just a white-washed church where candles flicker, making worried shadows on the wall, where the black-clad priest is an authority and nothing else matters except that relating to God. The same bare walls and ascetic figures appear in several of Bergman's films. Also, Dreyer's way of using actor Maria Renée Falconetti's face in the silent movie classic *La Passion de Jeanne d'Arc* is constantly repeated by Ingmar Bergman, placing the camera in a way that the actor's face is in focus instead of the room or context, and so it is through the shifting expressions of the face the psychological drama unfolds.

In *The Seventh Seal*, Ingmar Bergman refines the themes of faith, doubt, and anxiety about death. A knight, Antonius Block, is on his way home from the crusades. He is tired of life and travels through a landscape devastated by the plague. There he meets Death, literally. Death wants to take him immediately, but agrees to play a game of chess first. The knight longs to do one good deed before his life is over and when his skill as a chess player gives him a certain deferral from death, he uses it to save a young family from the plague.

The title of the film is from the Book of Revelation and refers to a biblical text about God's silence — where is God in times when the human being is vulnerable, in times of anxiety and doom? How does someone, who longs for God, bear a higher power that only communicates through silence? The theme recurs in several films. In *Cries and Whispers*, the priest says:

If you'd happen to meet God over there, in the other country. If it would happen that he turns his face towards you. If you then would happen to speak a language that this God understands. If you'd be able to talk to this God — if so, please pray for us.

But the image of Death in a black cape and hood?

Bergman himself said that he was primarily inspired by the painter Albrecht Dürer's image of Death and a knight riding together in a forest, as well as by the medieval church painter Albertus Pictor. In Täby church, close to Stockholm, there is a monumental picture of Death playing chess. But none of these figures are dressed in black or expose bone-white faces.

The Bergman expert Maaret Koskinen has found the presence of the black-dressed figure in an early stage in Bergman's imagery. In his twenties, Bergman wrote an Edgar Allan Poe-inspired short story about a woman who was murdered. There her neighbour describes the murderer: 'And his looks made me cold and scared. He was quite white in sight, and it looked as if there were no eyes there and he had a big slouch hat and a long black coat.'

Ingmar Bergman is said to personalise Swedish dysphoria and depression. From his collection of demons and anxiety, great art was created — but also something more. He turned death into an icon, a Protestant man in a black-and-white movie, a twin brother of the Norwegian Edvard Munch's figure in the painting *The Scream,* but calmer, more inexorable and obnoxious. The impression it made in pop culture is beyond all comparison. We drop the name of Death as if it were a celebrity without connection to our daily lives. Death is a meme, a re-occurring joke, a topic for a dinner conversation, a t-shirt motif, and a fridge magnet, and as such nothing much to worry about.

20

SCANDI NOIR

The ten books in the series *The Story of a Crime* by Maj Sjöwall and Per Wahlöö have been printed and reprinted, turned into films and then remakes, and all in all have created an image of a Sweden glimmering with dark self-criticism. The authors are celebrated for crime stories where the Swedish zeitgeist, as well as the welfare state, are dissected, thereby laying the foundation for the genre called Scandi Noir. The ten books about inspector Martin Beck, Gunvald Larsson, and the others have become an unlikely success. In their footsteps, a new generation of Swedish crime writers followed, like Henning Mankell and Stieg Larsson, each with millions of copies sold worldwide.

The fact that the duo Sjöwall and Wahlöö ushered in a new kind of social criticism to the crime genre is not news, on the contrary. That was the plan. Quoting Per Wahlöö, from 1967:

> Using the crime novel as a scalpel to cut up a society
> which is ideologically depleted and morally debatable —
> the so-called welfare society of a bourgeois nature — and
> simply find out who is responsible for what, and if there is
> anything left to be responsible for.

Sjöwall and Wahlöö appear increasingly disillusioned with each book they wrote. The cracks in the state's structure were all noted, their depths measured and shadows outlined. Something in Sweden was broken.

Even if the first three books in the series were slightly milder in their criticism, the following seven left no doubts in any reader's mind. In *The Laughing Policeman* from 1968, they mock the consumer society. The following year, they criticise Swedish immigration and integration policies in *The Fire Engine that Disappeared*. In *Murder at the Savoy*, the police authority itself is scorned; centralisation puts the authorities at a far remove from the citizenry, and a continuous theme is the idea that the elite protects itself. *The Locked Room* from 1972 deals with old people's care, and so on. To put it simply, things were better in the old days, in their eyes.

Once, there was another country, which now is almost lost. Here and there, the writers add elements of discrepancy in order to heighten the grade of contrast of the black-and-white image of Sweden. One example is the character Herrgott

Nöjd, a village policeman in the south of Sweden. His name could be translated into Mr-Good-and-Happy, a not very subtle contrast to the anonymous contemporary society with its multi-storey carparks and high suicide rates.

Major changes in the physical environment took place during Sweden's post-war era. Motoring increased, energy consumption increased, garbage mountains grew. Increasing pollution in the water and air was given great attention. Up until the mid-1960s, the politics of welfare had been focused on eliminating the problems of the old society by improving housing standards and expanding social welfare. Now, environmental issues became a crucial point of criticism towards the current system. Both Maj Sjöwall and Per Wahlöö were initially members of one of the several Swedish political groups trading under the name Communist Party (the SKP) before, in 1967, joining another, the Left Party Communists (VPK). In their crime novels, they took their Marxist ideology and examined the reality behind the housing estates and institutions of the welfare state. The image of a large-scale, centralised society emerges, where crimes are no longer discrete events in an otherwise calm world but are instead a normalised part of a brutal everyday life, and where the police no longer provide security but are an integral part of a society that is deteriorating from within.

When the middle class became much larger as a result of economic growth, with higher wages combined with an equalisation of income, it became dominant in both a political and cultural sense. As a result, a self-image emerged in which the Swedes lived in a homogeneous society. Sjöwall and Wahlöö, being part of the radical left, were strongly critical of the Social Democrats who had created this middle class at the expense of the workers. For instance, as a result, women were still oppressed — something even the good-natured Mr-Good-and-Happy considered a problem. In *Cop Killer* from 1974 he says, 'And I've always regarded women as regular people, essentially no different from me and men in general ... I've read a number of books and articles on women's lib, but most of it is nonsense. And the part that isn't nonsense is so obvious a Hottentot could understand it. Equal pay for equal work, for example, and sex discrimination.'

Perhaps Sjöwall and Wahlöö based their writing on the idea that the folkhem, the Swedish people's home, was unbreakable? Or were they really two revolutionaries who wanted to tear it all down in order to make place for a new order? Whatever the case, one can sum up their criticism in three words: disgust with modernity.

Their Scandi Noir style has since provided a blueprint for literary success; social awareness and criticism of the hypocrisy in society have become essential elements of today's crime fiction. Or should one say clichés? Whatever the case, it seems the world can't get enough of the bright Swedish model being ripped to pieces and found to be full of pain and darkness. Their series of ten novels have re-drawn the map of Sweden from moral template into crisis chart. And their way of thinking has been amplified beyond the pages of their books. The small-scale folkhem is still set against the mighty welfare state. Idyll against monolith. Public trust against corruption. Ordinary people against the elite. Domestic against foreign. Past against present.

Sjöwall and Wahlöö's leftist dystopia has become an established image of Sweden in some circles, perhaps even a cultural heritage that now is turned into politics by the right-wing populist party in the same way their representatives dress in Swedish folk costume. Politics based on nostalgia. It used to be so much better in the olden days.

CREATURES
OF DICTATORSHIP

'Politics is to aim for something', Olof Palme said, and he lived up to his words. Now and then a strong wave of Palme nostalgia sweeps over the public debate in Sweden. People seem to long for leaders who talk about ideals, change, and utopia, who strive to leave an indelible impression on the world.

He criticised the United States. He criticised the Soviet Union. He married a Czech woman in the late 1940s to help her out of a life under Communist oppression. Early on, he became one of the Swedish Prime Minister Tage Erlander's 'boys' — a young, well-placed, centrist man in power. But when he became Sweden's prime minister, he chose to focus on international matters. Was the folkhem, the people's home, furnished and complete by then? Did it bore him?

The late 1960s was a remarkable and agitating time. Above all, Vietnam became a place where the Cold War appeared in its most deadly and violent form, creating great human suffering as the superpowers fought each other by proxy.

Vietnamese communists and nationalists had fought alongside each other in order to get the French colonisers to leave. But then the country was divided. North Vietnam became a communist state while South Vietnam became a market economy supported by the United States. But within South Vietnam lurked the communist guerilla movement Việt Cộng, encouraged by North Vietnam to fight the South Vietnamese government. An election was planned for the people of Vietnam to decide on their future political method of reign, but the South Vietnamese leadership broke the agreement out of fear of a communist power takeover. With the superpowers meddling, the country was brought to war: North Vietnam supported the Việt Cộng, and was itself supported by China and the Soviet Union, who sent weapons, advisors, and military equipment. South Vietnam, on the other hand, received weapons, soldiers, and advisors from the United States and support from South Korea, Australia, and Thailand.

No one could go unaffected by the Vietnam War. It reached people all over the world through massive television footage and intensive news reporting, and the war became a major issue in the left-wing movement that made itself heard in the west. Also in Sweden.

There, the Social Democratic government of Tage Erlander was concerned the war would generate support at the polls for the Swedish Communists and thereby threaten a Social Democratic victory in the forthcoming parliamentary elections. One had to capture this 'youth revolt' and channel it. The solution was Olof Palme.

By taking part in an anti-war demonstration in Stockholm in 1968, Palme became an internationally renowned name overnight, not so much for what he said but because he walked side by side with Nguyen Tho Chan, the North Vietnamese ambassador to the Soviet Union. Palme's action aroused strong criticism from the United States, but that particular criticism was considered vital by the Social Democrats, who had indeed aspired to it in order to prevent voters from turning to the Swedish Communist Party.

The strategy worked: the Social Democrats won the election in 1968 with a total of 50.1 per cent of the votes. Its foreign policy was considered to be the key to the success, especially the party's strong position concerning Vietnam. In January 1969, Sweden was the first country in the world to recognise North Vietnam as an independent state. In October of the same year, Olof Palme was elected new party leader. He also became Sweden's prime minister.

The war in Vietnam officially came to end in 1975. Approximately 1.3 million people had died. Of these, 444,000 were Vietnamese soldiers and 282,000 were soldiers of other nationalities. The rest — 627,000 people — were Vietnamese civilians: children, women, and men.

That same year, Olof Palme created another significant diplomatic crisis when he attacked the leadership of Czechoslovakia, where the Communist regime imprisoned and persecuted socialists:

> The Interior Minister held a meeting the other day with the Chief of Police and Intelligence, stating that the authorities should do everything to expose and purge reactionary groups and individuals, and at the right time and without compromise stop their activities. Thus speak the creatures of dictatorship.[15]

Several of Palme's heavily ideological and sharp statements have left traces that still reverberate in Sweden. Under his leadership there was a major change in Swedish foreign policy, with Palme's condemnation of the US in Vietnam the starting point.

Up until then, Swedish foreign policy had been characterised by a policy of restraint. In the UN General Assembly,

---

15   Olof Palme's speech on 20 April 1975 https://www.youtube.com/watch?v=ypDRfGmvLm8

Sweden's votes rarely differed from the other Western states'. In the general international debate, Sweden's voice was not heard more than others. As a country 'free of alliances', Sweden instead became a buffer state between the two major power blocks. All that changed with Palme, with his political aims and visions.

He spoke about the 'Third World' — the poor countries that neither belonged to the communist block nor the western world — and argued that Sweden had a moral responsibility towards the people there. Economic and social injustice must be eradicated worldwide. Unless the rich world took responsibility, poverty and injustice would cause the third world to explode into conflict and suffering. The right to self-determination was another central idea of Palme's; he described nationalism and nationalist aspirations as a 'storm wave' that would wash out the colonisers.

These were the years when the basic ideals of Swedish international aid were developed, and Palme's ideas were highly influential in the process. The aid should have the purpose of improving living conditions for poor people worldwide through economic growth, economic and social equality, economic and political independence, as well as increased democracy. Interestingly enough, Olof Palme created a built-in contradiction in his support of North Vietnam, a country that wasn't in the least democratic. In that case, he prioritised the issue of independence, something that proved to be a pattern. In the choice between combating colonialism and promoting democracy, Palme's preference was usually not the democratic one. From his point of view, colonialism was the main enemy, and Swedish foreign policy under Palme's command defended the right to self-determination of small states. Not surprisingly, he is the Swedish politician who has by far the most streets and squares in the world named after him.

Sweden got the nickname 'the darling of the third world' and its foreign policy displayed plenty of moral confidence. At the very heart of it was the idea of it being a fundamental human obligation to extend a helping hand to the ones in need, as well as the belief that Sweden ought to show moral leadership. In Palme's own words, from 1968:

> Our face towards the world must be characterised by
> the same solidarity with the poor and oppressed that
> was the driving force when the workers' movement was
> formed in the old, poor Sweden, and guided our efforts
> to transform Swedish society on the basis of equality and
> righteousness.

Since then, it has been a well-founded Swedish position that Sweden is — and should be — a country that takes the lead in addressing the moral dilemmas of the world. The 1996

Declaration of Foreign Affairs states that Sweden should be a leader in world aid and humanitarian efforts. Furthermore, Sweden sees itself as a leading player within the UN and in contributing to peace and security throughout the world. The commitment to disarmament and the fight against weapons of mass destruction also remains a constant. And with membership of the EU, Sweden gradually began to emerge as a leading player in the eastward enlargement of the Union and in efforts to strengthen the EU's crisis management and peace promotion capabilities.

When the conservative alliance of four parties won the Swedish election in 2010, they all desired to uphold a political identity based on being a nation that exerted moral leadership in the world. Their 2013 Foreign Declaration actually stated that 'Sweden is a humanitarian superpower'. And that flattering self-portrait remains untouched and unmodified to this day.

22

NEVER VIOLENCE

It is virtually impossible to itemise all the traces of Astrid Lindgren visible in Swedish culture, so numerous are they. The mother of Pippi Longstocking, Emil of Lönneberga, and The Brothers Lionheart has impregnated the language as well as the collective way of thinking; her books are read by every parent, her songs are sung by every child. She has injected her readers with her own childhood. It's as if you become Astrid Lindgren by reading Astrid Lindgren.

Not to mention the uncountable literary references — without Pippi Longstocking, for instance, there would be no Lisbeth Salander. But there is more to it than that.

When Astrid Lindgren in 1976 realised that the state demanded 102 per cent of her income in marginal tax rate, she protested by writing a short story in one of the newspapers, ironically criticising the government. The following debate led to the first social democratic loss of political power in forty years.

A few years later, she initiated a debate about livestock farming, describing the lives of the animals in a way that made every meat-eater cry: cows that never see the light of day, heavily stressed pigs in small stalls, and hens so cramped that they tore and pecked each other to pieces. With a strong public opinion behind her, Astrid Lindgren got the Agriculture Minister to change the law and the working practices for the better.

She made herself a link between the old agrarian society and the new urban life, getting her readers to remember her own childhood memories. The depictions of everyday life on the farm in southern Sweden thus became a collective memory. She connected the yesterdays with the present, the rural Sweden with the urban, and older generations with younger during a time when past and present, country and city, and different generations slipped away from each other because of the speed of Swedish modernisation. She was the storyteller who held bewitching history lessons. And yet, despite all these accomplishments, Astrid Lindgren's most decisive action of all came in 1978.

But first let's return to the year of 1968, when a girl named Heike-Maria was born in Germany. The mother was in her early twenties and was abandoned by the father just a couple of months after the child was born. The baby girl stayed with her grandparents. After a while, the young mother met Marty, an American soldier. He had served in Vietnam and now worried he would have to return for a second round. He wanted to desert.

Heike-Maria's mother told her parents that she and Marty were planning to go on a weekend trip away, and she packed a bag and collected her daughter. Heike-Maria was now three years old. The young couple and the child drove randomly around Europe, looking for a country willing to receive a US Army deserter. Sweden turned out to be just the place. Through social services, Marty got an apartment north of Stockholm where they settled down.

Heike-Maria. In the Swedish newspapers of the time, she was just called Maria. The attorney counted over two hundred bruises on her three-year-old body, including on the genitals. Her mother had written letters to the grandparents back in Germany, reporting that everything was fine. Marty demanded unconditional obedience, she wrote, and wanted to be called 'daddy' but that it wasn't a problem as Heike-Maria was an obedient child, she called him 'daddy'.

The last day of the child's life was one of torture. It is hardly possible to read her mother's testimony in the police interrogations that followed, not to mention the statement from the pathologist. The three-year-old was forced to stand in a corner of a room for a whole night. When she seemed to be falling asleep, she was awakened, forced to vomit, forced to run. Three palm-sized patches on her head showed where hair was torn out. Marty told the police the child had to be punished for wetting the bed and when she had been shocked by the punishment, she had needed a 'counter shock'. Marty told the police he might have overreacted.

The Swedish press reported on the child's death, and covered the following trial. Suddenly there was a debate about parents' right to discipline children, which went on throughout 1971. Many defended the right to correct their children in a physical way; discipline was a part of upbringing and what would happen if the child wasn't 'brought up properly'? The Bible, as well as tradition, were invoked. The government responded by setting up an inquiry into children's rights. Yet, still nothing much happened. Not until seven years later, when Astrid Lindgren stepped in.

In October 1978, Astrid Lindgren was to be awarded the prestigious German Booksellers' Peace Prize in Frankfurt at that year's Book Fair. But when the organisers read her speech in advance, they got worried. It was all about peace beginning at home, that children ought to be raised with love and respect and not violence and coercion. The child who is treated lovingly by its parents learns to respond to the outside world in the same way, Astrid Lindgren planned to say.

It was controversial to interfere with the private sphere of family life, and the speech was considered so challenging that the organisers asked her not to give it. Astrid Lindgren replied that if she wasn't allowed to speak freely, she wouldn't come to the award ceremony. A representative of the prize committee was sent to Sweden to convince her to change the speech, but the Germans had to give in. Astrid Lindgren delivered her speech exactly as she wanted, demanding there be no violence towards children.

How can one avoid feeling despondent on hearing the current outcry advocating a return to old authoritarian methods? The clamour is coming from various places throughout the world at the moment. People are demanding 'a more rigorous approach' and 'tighter reins', and believe this will help to eradicate the youthful vices that are blamed on too much freedom and too little strictness in their upbringing. This is in fact an attempt to drive out the Devil with the aid of Beelzebub, and in the long run can only lead to more violence, and greater and more dangerous gaps between the generations. The 'more rigorous approach' being demanded might possibly have a superficial effect that its advocates could interpret as an improvement. Until they are eventually forced to accept that violence gives birth to more violence — as it has always done.[16]

Her speech had a huge impact and reignited the Swedish conversation. The debate that had started with the murder of Heike-Maria now matured into action. New legislation was proposed. The following year, 1979, Sweden became the first country in the world to ban all forms of psychological and physical violence towards children.

Ten years later, the UN General Assembly adopted the Convention on the Rights of the Child, which confirms children's rights, declaring their inviolable right to freedom of information and religion, and to free education, play, rest, and leisure. Today, fifty-two countries ban corporal punishment in the home. Thanks to Astrid Lindgren's intervention, the death of three-year old Heike-Maria on 14 March 1971 came to change the world.

---

16 Lindgren, Astrid, 'Never Violence!' Translated by Laurie Thompson. *Swedish Book Review* (2007) https://www.swedishbookreview.com/article-2007-2-never-violence.asp

23

THE BRIDGE

In the imagery of film, the subconscious is often symbolised by water while land denotes tangible reality. This is why one vignette after the other in almost every television series or film with any claim on telling some kind of searching psychological story begins with sequences depicting water and land. Sensibility contra sense, chaos contra control.

Sometimes the scene is filmed from above, the camera placed in a drone flying over beaches or following a river. Sometimes the camera is placed in the water, often just where the water's surface meets the air, in a heavy-handed metaphor of death, life, and the thin line in between.

The bridge is above all that. It is static but represents motion. It stands on solid ground, yet is beyond land. At the same time, it's connected to the water but still separated from it. With its arc, its reach, and its pillars, it conjoins two worlds that have previously been apart.

> There'll be no bridge. There'll be no bridge. I feel there will be no bridge. Because when we have crushed it, we'll blow it up and when we've blown it up we'll have a go again!

Accompanied by a drummer beating his drum out of time, the anti-bridge-activists chanted their protest to the tones of 'Bei mir bist du schön'. This was in the early 1990s and they were certain that the whole idea of a bridge between Sweden and Denmark was out of rhythm, a project for a future that had already passed into history. To build an enormous thing for transporting cars when trains were the graceful, efficient, and environmentally correct way to travel, was sheer madness. The concrete building site symbolised an immobile power structure. The government must come to its senses and prove that it didn't consist of old fossils, the anti-bridge-activists demanded at huge demonstrations.

A man interviewed on the radio was concerned about this thing called integration between Copenhagen and Malmö. Should people commute? he asked. He didn't approve of the idea. Instead jobs ought to be placed where people lived. 'There is nothing positive in having people unnecessarily transported back and forth.'

In Malmö, the opponents clung to the construction site of the bridge's foundations to stop the work progressing. In 1998, the leader of the Centre Party, Olof Johansson, left his post in protest. The bridge would be a danger to the environment, too expensive, and unnecessary, he argued. The plans to connect Sweden with Denmark created divisions in the Social Democratic Party, as well. Opponents argued that the bridge would prevent acidic water from reaching the Baltic Sea, and this would adversely affect the reproduction of the cod. The bridge would also interfere with the wandering sill and the dredging would damage the environment. The Social Democrat Anna Lindh was a harsh opponent but when she agreed to become Minister for the Environment, the whole project became her responsibility. On 1 July 2000 the bridge opened.

And now?

Well, the bridge didn't turn out to be such a blessing as imagined. Certainly, around 70,000 people commute over the bridge every day, about half of them by car, the other half by train. However, integration between Denmark and Sweden is still slow, due to structural barriers, such as differing tax rules and high housing prices.

On the other hand, it didn't turn out as badly as the activists had imagined. The surfaces of the concrete pillars under water now constitute the habitat for about 160 tonnes of blue mussels, which contribute to the purification of the water. Blue mussels are also a very important food for birds, especially eider ducks. The influx of water does not seem to have been affected. On the artificial island of Pepparholmen, nearly three hundred plant species have settled and up to thirteen bird species breed. Some unusual insect and spider species have been found and the rare green-speckled toad has established itself.

As far as the Danish-Swedish TV-series is concerned, it has been sold to 160 countries, according to Wikipedia. The bridge is a transgressing of borders, a change of mental state as well as a change of a geographical one. It is static, it is motion. It combines and expands. And nowadays quite a few of us tend to quote Saga Norén, saying: 'I'm not unstable. I'm just different.'

24

OPEN YOUR HEARTS

The Scandinavian model is built on the presumption that as many people as possible have jobs and thereby contribute to the common good. Buzzwords are freedom, equality, and taxation. The Swedish way is no exception to the rule.

That means there is one specific question that ought to engage everyone, regardless of political inclination, and it ought to be mandatory homework for anyone striving for political and economic power: what happens to the common welfare if a larger group of people does not work?

Now and then someone touches upon the subject in public conversation, but then backs off. For example, it's a well known fact that Sweden has an ageing population. How can the younger generations possibly work long and hard enough to pay the amount of tax required to support all future retirees? Should the retirement age not be increased, shouldn't the ageing have to provide for themselves for a few more years? It is a very real and serious problem across many developed nations, but nobody in Sweden seems particularly engaged; neither journalists, politicians, nor commentators on social media. It never gets heated, nobody is the target of hate speech on the subject, nobody is threatened or stalked for discussing demographics.

Nevertheless, the Swedish Model has a weak point, an in-built conundrum. If not enough people work, how will the state be able to acquire enough funds to maintain the good society citizens have become used to? The dilemma could very well have been debated in the early 1990s, when the number of employed in Sweden decreased by over half a million people. It would have been perfectly in keeping to question if the welfare state was at risk. But no one did, no one would or could declare or define this possible threat. Instead, they debated social benefits and focused mainly on fraud and the failures of the system. Hunting down benefit cheats or formulating a fundamental critique of a system that was 'too generous' dominated the debate completely. Hundreds of thousands were out of work, the welfare state's dilemma was already activated, but not a word was spoken in public about it. News reports, opinion polls, and election campaigns — they all left a void in the public debate.

The welfare state can of course be threatened in many different ways, but if no one even acknowledges the existence of a threat, it remains diffuse, muddled, and ready to be used by anyone who chooses, and in any way. And there we are — the dilemma has been hijacked. Today, the threat to common welfare is associated with immigration and refugees, seemingly definitively and inarguably.

Maybe the then Prime Minister Fredrik Reinfeldt wanted to change all that, in August 2014? Perhaps his speech was a way to regain lost territory in the public debate, to take control of how the dilemma was put into words? Maybe he also strived for transparency of the state of affairs. Whatever the reason, it was time to start campaigning for the coming election and Fredrik Reinfeldt gathered press and audience in a central square in Stockholm to give a speech. It turned out the to be the end of one chapter and the beginning of the present:

There are now refugees in numbers similar to the years of the Balkan crisis in the early 1990s. Therefore, I now appeal to the Swedish people for patience. I ask you to open your hearts in order to recognise people in a strong state of stress as their lives are under threat. They are fleeing to Europe. Towards freedom, towards improved living conditions. Be open. Be tolerant, even when people say that 'there will be too many', 'it will be difficult', 'it will be hard'. Be tolerant and prove you remember that we've done it before. We have seen people flee from stress,

escape oppression, people who have since entered our
society, learned the Swedish language, got a job, and are
now contributing to a better and freer Sweden.

There is something honourable in these words. They
display confidence in the voters and a faith in them to make
decisions that might cause them discomfort in the short term
for the long-term good. Fredrik Reinfeldt put words to the
dilemma, but it was too late. Instead of opening Swedish
hearts, he became the first established politician to define
the welfare state's dilemma in the same way as the immigra-
tion-critical did, placing the common welfare in one hand and
refugees in the other.

There were consequences. According to a 'Diversity
Barometer', a survey conducted by Gävle University, a clear
majority of the population were favourable to the idea that
people should have the same social rights, regardless of whether
they were born in Sweden or abroad. In the 2016 survey, however, the percentage recorded as favourable declined from 77
per cent to 55 per cent, the lowest figure since measurements
began in 2005.

Reinfeldt's speech turned out to be a crucial turning point.
Up until then, welfare had been weighed against tax cuts. But
from 1 o'clock on Saturday 16 August 2014, welfare was officially to be weighed on society's scales against immigration.

In one instant, the political debate changed and now was all about the costs of receiving refugees. The speech became an important explanation for the great success of the right-wing populist Swedish Democrats in the 2014 elections.

Examining social media from this period gives evidence for the thesis. Up until 16 August, the Swedish terms for 'immigration' and/or 'refugee reception' were mentioned on average in 745 tweets each week. After the speech, 2,438 tweets per week used the terms.

Checking the newspapers provides a similar result. The number of articles that linked the concepts 'welfare' and 'immigration' increased from 108 in the month of July, to 926 in the month of August — after the speech.

The open-your-hearts speech caused Fredrik Reinfeldt not only the loss of the general elections, governmental power and his job as leader of the conservative party (Moderaterna). It also changed the tone and vocabulary of the public debate in Sweden. If responsible politicians and opinion makers without an anti-immigrant agenda had been prepared to discuss the dilemma and had exposed the structural weakness of the welfare state earlier, Reinfeldt's speech could have had a different meaning, the present could have had another colour and — who knows? — so could the future.

25

ZLATAN, THE SWEDE

Trying to define Swedishness requires the embrace of a paradox. On the one hand, there are idealised stories of independent, individualistic, and unbreakable Vikings or the strong-willed Vasa-family who are said to have founded the kingdom of Sweden. The myth they all carry through time can be concluded in the Swedish saying: 'He who stands alone is strong.'

On the other hand, the prevailing idea of the perfect society today is one that places at the centre the loyal team. In building the welfare state, the story of collective effort has been at the centre of the narrative. Everyone pays taxes. Everyone contributes. Everyone joins in. Everyone benefits. Without the collective — the workers' movement, the trade unions, the temperance movement, the awakening movement, the women's liberation movement, without the collective agreements in the labour market — the Swedish welfare state would not be so strong and stable.

The Swedish Model is based on an agreement between state and individual. In case of weakness, illness, or distress, the individual in Sweden can turn to the state, who then gives a direct response in the form of grants, pensions, and insurance systems. It frees the individual from family dependence, class consciousness, or the humiliation of seeking charity from private benefactors. All state grants (except for parental leave) are now directly linked to the individual citizen. In Germany, they are more often linked to the family, while the individual in the United States turns to her or his social networks or charities to receive aid in crises, not to the state. So, in Sweden there are two narratives, two stories. The one about a strong individual, the other about a strong collective. In between, we find Zlatan Ibrahimović.

In the early days of Zlatan's career, he was repeatedly described as a sulky kid, self-centred and, worst of all, a terrible team player.

In the year of 2000, Zlatan was still an unknown but unusually talented footballer, without even a nickname. In an interview with a Swedish newspaper, he claimed that he would be a professional in the prestigious Italian club Inter Milan within just a few years, and was described as a 'rough diamond, a Hulk, a different type of football player'.

The Swedish journalist Agneta Furvik has scrutinised the Swedish media's encounters with Zlatan during the first years of his growing fame and the pattern is clear. He is overwhelmingly often characterised as someone who stands out, who differs from the rest of the players in the Swedish national team. Adjectives such as 'cocky', 'cheeky', 'impulsive', 'spontaneous', and 'individualistic' are the words most often used to describe him, all of them synonyms to the equally reoccuring 'un-Swedish'.

In the arena of sport, issues of national identity are just as important as the beauty of the game and sometimes they take over completely — nothing new there. But in Sweden something has changed radically since that day in 2000 when the nineteen-year-old Zlatan was interviewed. A shift of paradigm. Sweden before the year 2000 was quite simply another country.

The list of fundamental changes in society is long, and the direction of travel has been entirely one-way, from public sector to private, from state responsibility to individual, from a structure based on the collective to a structure based on individualism. The wave of change has swept over the educational system, changed the terms for retirement, created a decentralisation of the labour market, changed the rules for dismissing people, and initiated the selling of public housing to private owners — to mention just some of the transformations.

When a conservative alliance came to power in 2006, the shift was speeded up. Individualism was the way to freedom, they declared. The powers of the public sphere and the state itself should decrease, and the individual should gain more influence: this was their operating principle.

At a press conference in 2011, the prime minister was asked about the 400,000 Swedes who had been kicked out of the unemployment insurance fund since he won the election — how would they be able to support themselves if there was a major recession? Prime Minister Reinfeldt replied, 'One gets support and help from one's parents, partner or otherwise. If the worst comes to the worst, there are other social security systems to catch you should you fall.'

An unambiguous proof of a changed system. The Swedish welfare system was no longer valid for all Swedish citizens. Now was the time of the individual. And Zlatan was never again accused of being a bad team player in an un-Swedish way. On the contrary. Prior to the World Cup qualification match against Portugal in 2013, Zlatan Ibrahimović held a press conference in his role as team captain for the national football team and managed to portray his personality as well as express the new Swedish times in one single sentence: 'If I am to succeed, the whole team must do their job.'

The following year, Zlatan was the main character in a commercial by Volvo titled 'Made by Sweden featuring Zlatan'.[17]

---

17 https://www.youtube.com/watch?v=cbvdzQ7uVPc

There, he recites the national anthem with slightly changed lyrics. (The word 'North' was replaced by 'Sweden' in the phrase 'I want to live, I want to die in Sweden'.) The film consists of winter landscapes, mountains, rivers, forests, and open spaces. The car model it is meant to promote doesn't account for more than 25 per cent of the film's total time. Instead, the focus is on Zlatan. He pulses in deep, white snow, goes deer hunting, takes a winter bathe in a lake covered in ice, and hangs out with his family in a rural cottage. No collective, no social network nor friend as far as one can see.

Could Volvo have shot the same movie in 2000? Of course not. Times have changed. Alone is strong. Zlatan is strong. Zlatan is Volvo. Volvo is Sweden. Sweden is individualistic. In other words: Swedish society has caught up with Zlatan Ibrahimović. The journalists who portrayed him in the first years of his career were all wrong. He wasn't un-Swedish. He was simply Swedish before everyone else was.

ACKNOWLEDGEMENTS

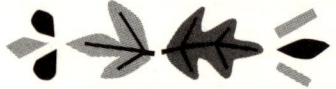

As Isaac Newton once said, inspired by Bernard of Chartres, 'If I have seen further it is by standing on the shoulders of giants.'

That goes for this book as well. The thoughts, research and writings of other hard-working people laid the foundation for my essays about Sweden. Lawmakers, hymnologists, poets, and researchers in all sorts of fields have contributed to such an extent that I hereby thank them all collectively. No one mentioned but no one forgotten — as we say in Sweden.

Special thanks to my publisher, Philip Gwyn Jones, who encouraged me to transform this originally Swedish book about Sweden into a special English edition, and to all you brilliant people at Scribe, London, for your support and skill. Thank you.

—Elisabeth Åsbrink, December 2018

SMÖRGÅSBORD BEOWULF SAUNA

N'S RIGHTS SAUNA LAGOM OWULF

NAZIS DESIGN SOCIALISM

AUNA VIKINGS BERGMAN WOMEN'S RIGHTS SAUNA

NEUTRALITY SMÖRGÅSBORD BEOWULF SAUNA DESIGN NEUTRALITY

EQUALITY VIKINGS VIKINGS TOLERANCE

NATURE ABBA LAGOM IKEA

TROLLS BEOWULF NAZIS

BEOWULF SEXUAL LIBERATION TROLLS SAUNA NATURE NEUTRALITY

NEUTRALITY ABBA DESIGN SAUNA

ABBA EQUALITY SAUNA ABBA TOLERANCE

NEUTRALITY NEUTRALITY TOLERANCE IKEA SAUNA

IKEA SOCIALISM BERGMAN ABBA

WOMEN'S RIGHTS NATURE NAZIS VIKINGS

DESIGN LAGOM SMÖRGÅSBORD IKEA

SAUNA ABBA VIKINGS

TROLLS SAUNA

TOLERANCE BEOWULF TOLERANCE

OM NAZIS TROLLS EQUALITY DESIGN

NATURE BERGMAN ABBA SEXUAL LIBERATION NEUTRALITY

EQUALITY ABBA EQUALITY WOMEN'S RIGHTS

VIKINGS WOMEN'S RIGHTS TOLERAN

OCIALISM SAUNA IKEA NATURE

N'S RIGHTS SOCIALISM ABBA DESIGN